DIAMOND
ASSAMESE LEARNING & SPEAKING COURSE

ASSAMESE
অসমীয়া

DIAMOND ASSAMESE LEARNING & SPEAKING COURSE THROUGH ENGLISH

By
Debajit Saikia

প্ৰকাশক ঃ
ডায়মণ্ড পকেট বুকচ (প্ৰাঃ) লিমিটেড
X-30, ওখলা ইণ্ডাষ্ট্ৰিয়েল এৰিয়া (ফেজ-2)
নতুন দিল্লী--110 020
ফোন 011-41611861
ফেক্স 011-41611866

সংস্কৰণ ঃ 2013

DIAMOND ASSAMESE LEARNING & SPEAKING COURSE THROUGH ENGLISH : By DEBAJIT SAIKIA :

A Word from the Publishers

With a view to strengthening the unity of our country, we proudly offer the book series "LEARN THE NATIONAL LANGUAGES." The series with help the people of our country to learn any Indian language other than their mother tongue through the medium of English.

This book 'Diamond Assamese Learning and Speaking Course' is a part of the series.

This book has three parts. The first part will cover the basic knowledge about the Assamese language and the rest two parts will help the learner not only to converse in Assamese, but in the field of practical application of the language also.

We hope this series will bring together the people of various parts of our country and will be able to promote national integrity and unity.

—Diamond pocket Books

PREFACE

One of the 18 recognised National Languages of India, Assamese has its origin way back in the 7th century A.D., but it assumed its present form only in the latter half of the nineteenth century. Since then it has been flourishing as a modern Indian language under the penmanship of a good number of litterateurs and linguists.

It has been our sincere effort to present a brief but compact course on learning Assamese through English. We have tried to incorporate almost all the important aspects of the language in a lucid style so that the learners can have a clear idea about the nature and use of the language. However, with regard to pronounciation and tone, it is always advisable to consult, whenever possible, a person whose mother tongue is Assamese—a fact which is true of any other language.

We welcome the readers' response about the effectiveness of this course.

—COMPILER

INDEX

Lesson-1
Alphabet
বৰ্ণমালা

Vowels (Swarabarna)

There are 11 (eleven) vowels in Assamese :-

অ	আ	ই	ঈ
a, o	a, aa	i	i, ee
উ	ঊ	ঋ	
u	u, oo	ri	
এ	ঐ	ও	ঔ
e, ae	oi	o	ou

Vowels are of two kinds :-

(a) Short (hraswa) vowels, and
(b) Long (dirgha) vowels.
(a) Short vowels are : অ (a, o), ই (i), উ (u)
(b) Long vowels are : আ (a, aa) ঈ (i,ee), ঊ (u, oo)

Read :-

উ অ এ ঈ ঋ ঊ ঔ আ
ও ঐ ই

Consonants (byonjon borno)

ক্	খ্	গ্	ঘ্	ঙ্
k	kh	g	gh	ng
ক	খ	গ	ঘ	ঙ
ko	kho	go	gho	ngo
চ	ছ	জ	ঝ	ঞ
so	so	jo	jho	no
ট	ঠ	ড	ঢ	ণ
to	tho	do	dho	no
ত	থ	দ	ধ	ন
to	tho	do	dho	no
প	ফ	ব	ভ	ম
po	pho	bo	bho	mo

য	ৰ	ল	ৱ
jo, zo	ro	lo	wo
শ	ষ	স	হ
*xo, sho	*xo, sho	*xo, so	ho
ক্ষ	ড়	ঢ়	য়
kkha	ra	rha	ya
ৎ	ং	ঃ	ঁ
t	ng	h	chandrabindu

* Please refer to Lesson No. 5 for pronunciation of these letters.

Read :

প	ৰ	•	শ	য
ম	ষ	ঢ়	ল	ং

ভ	ব	হ	ঃ	স
র	ফ	ৎ	ড়	য়
ন	ঢ	ঝ	খ	চ
ঠ	দ	জ	ড	ট
ক	ঙ	ণ	ছ	ত
ধ	গ	ঞ	থ	ঘ

Lesson-2

How to Write

(Begin from No. 1,2,3.......Serially)

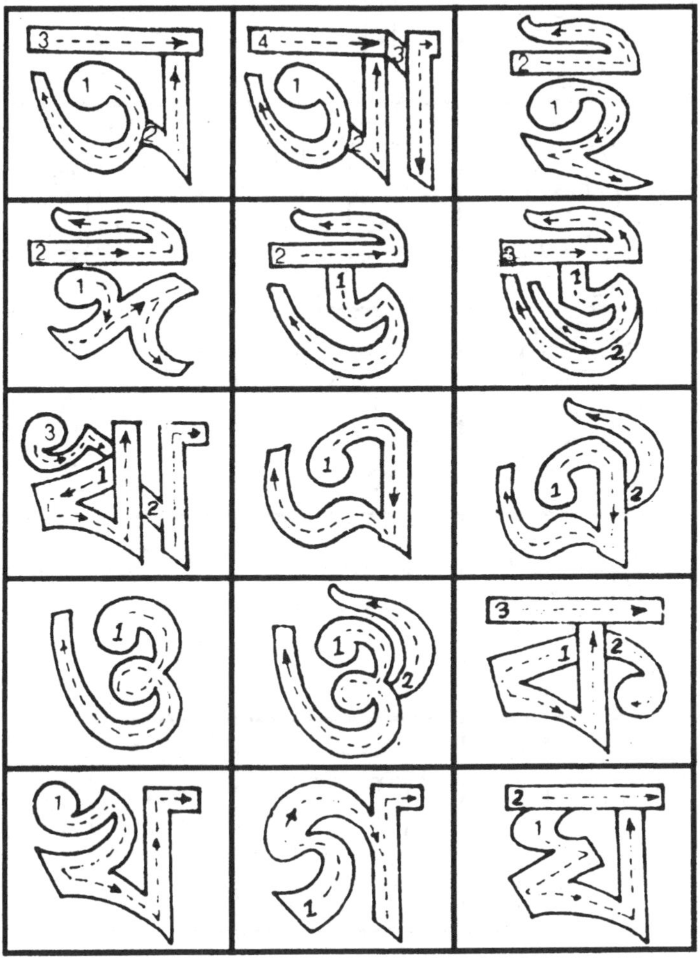

(Begin from No. 1,2,3.......Serially)

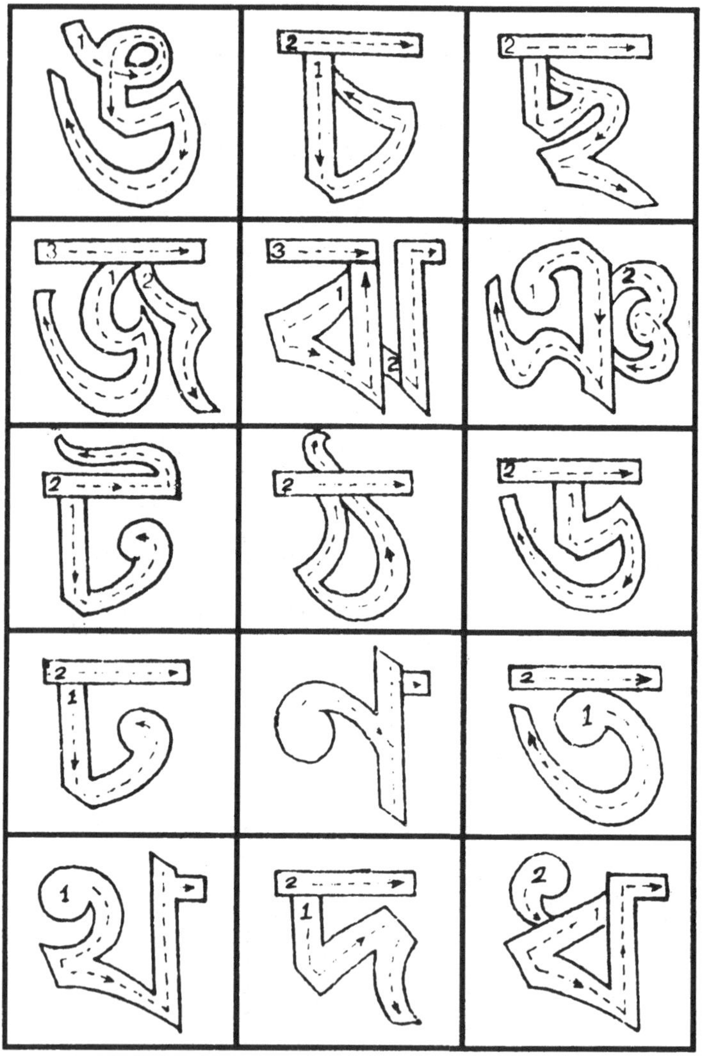

(Begin from No. 1,2,3.......Serially)

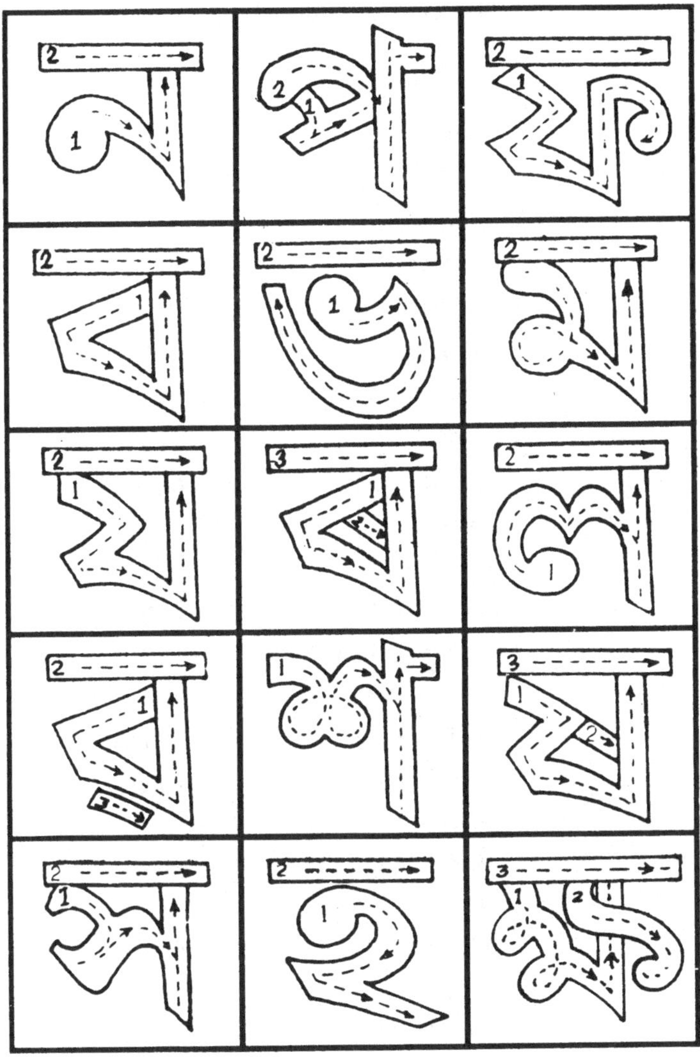

Lesson : 3

Reading and Writng

পঢ়া আৰু লিখা

অৰুণ	orun	sun
অনল	onol	fire
নৱ	nowo	new
দৰ্শন	dorxon	vision
মধুৰ	modhur	sweet
ক্ষণ	kkhyon	moment
আপোন	apon	own
মন	mon	mind
অজেয়	ojeyo	unconquerable
পণ	pon	oath

All vowels have their signs except 'অ' as follows :

আ (া)	দাদা (dada)	মামা (mama)
	Elder brother	(Maternal uncle)
ই (ি)	দিন (din)	ৰাতি (rati)
	Day	Night
ঈ (ী)	খুড়ী (khuri)	মামী (mami)
	Aunt	Maternal Aunt
উ (ু)	টুপী (tupi)	মুনি (muni)
	Hat	sage
ঊ (ূ)	ভূমি (bhumi)	পূজা (puja)

	Land	Worship
ঋ (ৃ)	বৃহৎ (brihot)	ঘৃণা (ghrina)
	Vast	Hatred
এ (ে)	বেশ (bex)	দেশ (dex)
	Dress	Country
ঐ (ৈ)	ঐশ্বৰ্য্য oishwarjya)	দৈৰ্ঘ্য (doirghyo)
	Wealth	Length
ও (ে া)	ওলোটা (olota)	কোমল (komol)
	Opposite	Soft
ঔ (ে ৗ)	সৌভাগ্য (xoubhagyo)	গৌৰব (gourob)
	Good-luck	Pride
ং	দংশন dongxon)	সিংহ (xingho)
	Bite	Lion
ঃ	নিঃশেষ (nihxex)	পুনঃ পুনঃ (punoh punoh)
	Finished/Eliminated	Repeatedly
ঁ	কাঁচি kansi)	হাঁচি (hansi)
	Sickle	Sneezing

ক	কা	কি	কী	কু	কূ	কৃ
ko	ka	ki	ki	ku	ku	kri
কে	কৈ	কো	কৌ	কং	কঃ	কঁ
ke	koi	ko	kou	kong	koh	kon
খ	খা	খি	খী	খু	খূ	খৃ
kho	kha	khi	khi	khu	khu	khri
খে	খৈ	খো	খৌ	খং	খঃ	খঁ
khe	khoi	kho	khow	khong	khoh	khon
গ	গা	গি	গী	গু	গূ	গৃ
go	ga	gi	gi	gu	gu	gri

গে	গৈ	গো	গৌ	গং	গঃ	গঁ
ge	goi	go	gow	gong	goh	gon
ঘ	ঘা	ঘি	ঘী	ঘু	ঘূ	ঘৃ
gho	gha	ghi	ghi	ghu	ghu	ghri
ঘে	ঘৈ	ঘো	ঘৌ	ঘং	ঘঃ	ঘঁ
ghe	ghoi	gho	ghow	ghong	ghoh	ghon

There are 5 consonants which change their original forms when they are combined with উ and ঊ। The 5 consonants are গ, ৰ, শ, স and হ। Their transformations are as follows :-

গ্ + উ = গু (গু)	গুণ gun) Quality
ৰ্ + উ = ৰু (ৰু)	ৰুটি (ruti) Bread (Roti)
ৰ্ + ঊ = ৰূ (ৰূ)	ৰূপ (rup) silver, beauty
স্ + উ = সু (সু)	সুকীয়া xukiya) separate
শ্ + উ = শু (শু)	শুদ্ধ xuddho) correct
হ্ + উ = হু (হু)	হুবহু hubohu) exactly

'হ' also takes a different form, when it is combined with ঋ;
হ্ + ঋ (ৃ) = হৃ (হৃ) হৃদয় (hridoi) heart.

Read :-

মা	(ma)	mother
দেউতা	(deuta)	father
পিতা	(pita)	father
মাতা	(mata)	mother
ভাই	(bhai)	younger brother
ভনী	(bhoni)	younger sister
দাদা	(dada)	elder brother
বাইদেউ	(baideu)	elder sister

ককাইদেউ	(kokaideu)	elder brother
নবৌ	(nobou)	didyrt-in-law (bhabhi)
খুড়া	(khura)	paternal uncle
খুড়ী	(khuri)	paternal aunt
মামা	(mama)	maternal uncle
মামী	(mami)	maternal aunt
বৰদেউতা	(bordeuta)	paternal uncle (elder to father
বৰমা	(borma)	paternal aunt
ককা	(koka)	grandfather
আইতা	(aita)	grandmother
ল'ৰা	(lora)	boy
ছোৱালী	(sowali)	girl
কিশোৰ	(kixor)	teenaged boy
কিশোৰী	(kixori)	teenaged girl
যুবক	(jubok)	youngman
যুবতী	(juboti)	young woman
প্ৰৌঢ়	(prourho)	middle aged man
প্ৰৌঢ়া	(prourha)	middle aged woman
বৃদ্ধ	(briddho))	old man
বৃদ্ধা	(briddha)	old woman
পকা কঁঠাল	(poka konthal)	ripe jackfruit
বগা বাঘ	(boga bagh)	white tiger
ক'লা কুকুৰ	(kola kukur)	black dog
নতুন জোতা	(notun jota)	new shoes
পুৰণা চোলা	(purona sola)	old shirt

ৰঙা ফিটা	(ronga phita)	red ribhon
মোৰ ভাই	(mor bhai)	my brother
তোমাৰ খুড়া	(tomar khura)	your uncle
তেওঁৰ দেউতাক	(teonr deutak)	his father
ভিতৰলৈ আহা	(bhitoroloi aha)	come in
বাহিৰতে ৰোৱা	(bahirote rowa)	wait outside
মূৰ্খ ছোৱালী	(murkho sowali)	foolish girl
চতুৰ মানুহ	(Sotur manuh)	clever man
মই ঘৰলৈ যাওঁ	(moi ghoroloi jawn)	I go home.
তুমি কথা কোৱা	(Tumi kotha kowa)	You talk.
তোমালোকে কি কৰা ?	(tomaloke ki kora?)	What do you do?
আমি নাটক কৰোঁ।	(ami natok koron)	We present plays.
আপুনি কি কৰে ?	(apuni ki kore?)	What do you do?
মই উপন্যাস লিখোঁ।	(moi uponyax likhon)	I write novels.

Lesson-4

Conjunct Letters যুক্তাক্ষৰ

য, ৰ, ল, ব, ন, and ম take their following forms, when joined to other consonants :-

য (্য) ঃ	ক্য	খ্য	গ্য	ঘ্য	চ্য
y	kya	khya	gya	ghya	sya, chya...etc.
ৰ (্ৰ) ঃ	ক্ৰ (ক্র)	খ্ৰ	গ্ৰ	ঘ্ৰ	ত্ৰ
r	kra	khra	gra	ghra	tra...etc.
ল (্ল) ঃ	ক্ল	গ্ল	ম্ল	প্ল	ল্ল
l	kla	gla	mla	pla	lla...etc.
ব (্ব) ঃ	ক্ব	জ্ব	ত্ব	দ্ব	ধ্ব ন্ব
w	kwa	jwa	twa	dwa	dhwa nwa...etc.
ন (্ন) ঃ	গ্ন	ঘ্ন	ন্ন	শ্ন	ক্ষ্ন
n	gna	ghna	nna	sna	khna...etc.
ম (্ম) ঃ	ত্ম	দ্ম	ন্ম	স্ম	
m	tma	dma	nma	sma....etc.	
ৰেফ (´) ঃ	ৰ্ক	ৰ্খ	ৰ্গ	ৰ্চ	ৰ্জ
r	rka	rkha	rga	rsa	rja...etc.

Practice :

বাক্য (bakyo)	খাদ্য (khadyo)
sentence	food
ঘ্ৰাণ (ghran)	প্ৰকৃতি (prokriti)
smell	nature
ক্লেশ (klex)	ম্লান (mlan)
trouble	faded
ঈশ্বৰ ishwar)	জ্বৰ (jwor)
God	fever

রুগ্ন (rugno)
sick
জন্ম (jonmo)
birth
মূৰ্খ (murkho)
foo!

অন্ন (onno)
food
আত্মা (atma)
soul
পাৰ্গত pargot)
skilled

precious jewel	মূল্যবান ৰত্ন	(mulyowan rotno)
hardworking villager	পৰিশ্ৰমী গাওঁবাসী	(porisromi gaonbaxi)
successful life	সাৰ্থক জীৱন	(xarthok jiwon)
Father of the world	বিশ্ব পিতা	(bishwo pita)
tired man	ক্লান্ত মানুহ	Klanto manuh)
broken health	ভগ্ন স্বাস্থ্য	(bhogno swasthyo)
saced motherland	পবিত্ৰ জন্মভূমি	(pobitro jonmohhumi)
unjust act	অন্যায় কাৰ্য	(onyai karjo)

Harder Conjuncts :

ক্ + ত = ক্ত (kta)
গ্ + ধ = গ্ধ (gdha)
ঙ্ + ক = ঙ্ক (ngka)
ঙ্ + ক্ষ = ঙ্ক্ষ (ngkha)
ঞ্ + জ = ঞ্জ (nja)
দ্ + দ = দ্দ (dda)
ব্ + দ = ব্দ (bda)
শ্ + চ = শ্চ (ssa)
হ্ + ম = হ্ম (hma)
ষ্ + প = ষ্প (spa)
ত্ + ৰ = ত্ৰ (tra)
ণ্ + ড = ণ্ড, ণ্ড (nda)
হ্ + ন = হ্ন (hna)

ক্ + .ক্ক, ক্ক (kka)
ক্ + ৰ = ক্ৰ, ক্ৰ (kra)
ত্ + ত = ত্ত (tta)
ঙ্ + গ = ঙ্গ, ঙ্গ (ngna)
ঞ্ + ছ = ঞ্ছ (nchha)
জ্ + ঞ = জ্ঞ (jna, gya)
দ্ + ধ = দ্ধ, দ্ধ (bdha)
ব্ + ধ = ব্ধ (bdha)
শ্ + ছ = শ্ছ (schha)
ষ্ + ক = ষ্ক (ska)
ত্ + থ = ত্থ (ttha)
ত্ + ৰ্, উ = ত্ৰু (tru)
ষ্ + ট = ষ্ট (sta)

স্ + ক = স্ক (ska)
স্ + থ = স্থ (stha)
ন্ + ত = ন্ত (nta)
স্ + ত = স্ত (sta)
স্ + প = স্প (spa)
ন্ + ত্ + উ = ন্তু (ntu)
স্ + ত্ + উ = স্তু (stu)

hibiscus	ৰক্তজবা	(roktojoba)
spy	গুপ্তচৰ	(guptsor)
south pole	দক্ষিণ মেৰু	(dokkhin meru)
northern hemisphere	উত্তৰ গোলাৰ্দ্ধ	(uttor golarddho)
naked truth	নগ্ন সত্য	(nogno xotyo)
old man	বৃদ্ধ লোক	(briddho lok)
Black Sea	কৃষ্ণ সাগৰ	(krisno xagor)
high ambition	উচ্চ আকাঙ্ক্ষা	(uchcho akangkha)
faithful servant	বিশ্বাসী লগুৱা	(bishwaxi loguwa)
trifling matter	তুচ্ছ কথা	(tuchchho kotha)
hot air	উষ্ণ বায়ু	(usno bayu)
national rising	জাতীয় উত্থান	(jatiyo utthan)
wicked nature	দুষ্ট প্ৰকৃতি	(dusto prokriti)
blind man	অন্ধ মানুহ	(ondho manuh)
fruitless effort	নিষ্ফল চেষ্টা	(nisphol sesta)
fickle minded girl	চঞ্চল ছোৱালী	(sonchol sowali)
bright star	উজ্জ্বল তৰা	(ujjwal tora)
well-behaved student	শিষ্টাচাৰী ছাত্ৰ	(xistasari satro)
latest invention	শেহতীয়া আৱিষ্কাৰ	(xehotiya awiskaar)

Practise :

A learned man is honoured everywhere

বিদ্বানে সকলোতে সন্মান পায়।

(bidwaane xokolote xonman pai)

The soul is immortal.

আত্মা অমৰ।

(atma omor)

The man is very tired.

মানুহজন বৰ ক্লান্ত

(manuhjon bor klanto)

The village people are hard-working. Villagers are hard working.

গাঁৱৰ মানুহ পৰিশ্ৰমী ।

(gawonr manuh porisromi)

Don't argue uselessly.

বৃথা তৰ্ক নকৰিবা।

(britha torko nokoriba)

The representatives have arrived.

প্ৰতিনিধিসকল আহি পালেহি।

(protinidhi xokol ahi palehi)

Idleness is the roof of all evils.

আলস্যই সকলো আপদৰ মূল।

(alosyoi xokolo apodor mul)

As you sow, so you reap.

যেনে কাম, তেনে ফল

(jaenae kam, taenae phol)

It is useless to argue with a fool.

মূৰ্খৰ লগত তৰ্ক কৰা বৃথা।

(murkhor logot torko kora britha)

Lesson : 5

Pronunciation উচ্চাৰণ

Vowel স্বৰবৰ্ণ (Swarabarna)

অ (o) is pronounced like English 'o' as in doll, hot, pot, cotton etc. Examples; মন (mon) mind, ঘৰ (ghor) house, ধন (dhon) money, ৰত্ন (rotno) jewel, মহৎ (mohot) noble etc.

Sometimes 'অ' is pronounced like 'o' in hope, note, rode etc. Examples are অধিকাৰ (odhikaar) right, অনুমতি (onumoti) permission, যদি (jodi) if, নকৰিবা (nokoriba) don't do etc. Sometimes this particular sound is indicated by a comma (') appearing on the top base, immediately following the concerned letter. For example, ল'ৰা (lora) **boy.** অ'ত ত'ত (ot tot) here and there, হ'ব (hobo) it will do etc.

'আ' (a) has the long sound of English 'a' as in words like large, charge, calm, chart, and the short sound of 'u' as in but, cut, hut, sun etc. Usually when 'আ' is the only vowel in word. It is pronounced long. Examples আম (aam) mango, আঠ (aath) eight, কাম (kaam) work, যাম (jaam) I shall go etc. Otherwise it is mostly pronoujnced short. examples : কথা (kotha) speech, পঢ়া (porha) read, নকৰিবা (nokoriba) don't do, আমাৰ

(amar) our, দেউতাৰ (deutar) father's etc.

'ই' (i) — has the short sound of English 'i' as in pin, bin, bit, mill, etc. Examples : নিয়ম (niyom) rule, ইয়াত (iyat) here, কৰিম (korim) I shall do, etc.

ঈ (i,ee) — Is pronounced long, like 'ee' in meet, feet, etc., when it appears as the only vowel in a word. Examples : গীত (geet) song, বীৰ (beer) hero, তীৰ (teer) arrow etc. Otherwise it is pronounced short, as in জীৱন (jiwon) life, পক্ষী (pokkhi) bird, etc.

উ (u) — has the short sound of English 'is' in put, pull, bull, etc. Examples : পুখুৰী (pukhuri) pond, কুকুৰ kukur) dog, উট (ut) camel etc.

ঊ (u, oo) — is pronounced long, like 'oo' in moon, root, loose, room etc., when it is the only vowel in a word, e.g., ৰূপ (roop) silver, ভূত (bhoot) ghost, দূৰ (door) distance etc. In other cases it is pronounced like উ (short), for example : ৰূপহী (rupohi) beautiful woman, উপকূল (upokul) coast, seashore, অনুকূল (onukul) favourable, etc.,

ঋ (ri) — resembles the sound of 'ri' in ritual, trim, friction, as in মৃত (mrito) dead, হৃদয় (hridoi) heart, বৃহৎ (brihot) big etc.

এ (e, ae) — is pronounced like the 'a' of cat, hat, bat, flat in words like এক (aek) one, লেতেৰা (laetaera) dirty, বেৰ (baer) wall etc. (This sound has been represented by the symbol 'ae' in this book). In some other words this vowel is pronounced like the ‘e’ of get, let, met, etc. Examples : কেতিয়া (ketiya) when, এদিন (edin) oneday, মেকুৰী (mekuri) cat etc.

ঐ (oi) There is no similar letter in English for this sound. It is a diphthong of ‘o’ (of অধিকাৰ) and ‘I’. Examples of this are : নৈতিক (noitik) moral, ঐতিহ্য (oitijyo) heritage, ঐক্য (oikyo) unity etc.

ও (o) This is perhaps the most difficult vowel in Assamese. There is no equivalent sound for it in English, although the letter ‘o’ has been used in this book to serve the purpose. While pronouncing ‘ও’, The lips become more rounded than what they are in case of ‘অ’। Examples are : কোন (kon) who, ওলা (ola) come out, or get out, ওলোটা (olota) opposite, গোল (gol) round, পোন (pon) straight etc.

ঔ (ou) is also a dipthong and is the combination of ‘অ’ (of অধিকাৰ) and ‘উ’. Examples : ঔষধ (ouxodh) medicine, মৌ (mou) honey, গৌৰৱ (gourov) pride, ঔদ্যোগিক (oudyogik) Industrial.

Consonants – ব্যঞ্জনবৰ্ণ (byonjon borno)

A consonant cannot be fully pronounced without the help of a vowel. (স্বৰবৰ্ণ) অ (o) remains inherent in every consonant (ব্যঞ্জনবৰ্ণ), as – ক (ক্ + অ) = k + o; খ (খ্ + অ) = kh + o; গ (গ্ + অ) + g + o, ঘ (ঘ্ + অ) = gh + o etc.

But when a consonant is not followed by any

	vowel, it is indicated somteimes by a holonto (্) below the letter and is written as ক্, খ্, গ্ etc.
ক (ko)	has the sound of the letter 'C' in words like committee, call, caution tc. Examples : কাম kaam) work, কেনেকৈ (kenekoi) how, কৰা (kora) do, কবিতা (kobita) poem etc.
খ (kho)	has the combined sound of English 'k' and 'h', as— খেল (khael) games, খৰাং (khorang) drought, etc.
গ (go)	has the sound of English 'g' in god, go, give etc; as— গাঁও (gaon) village, গৰম (gorom) hot, গধূলি (godhuli) evening etc.
ঘ (gho)	has the combined sound of 'g' and 'h' as— ঘড়ী (ghori) clock, ঘৰ (ghor) house, etc.
ঙ (ungo, ng)	has the nasal sound of English 'ng' in sing, ring, song, long etc. No word in Assamese begins with 'ঙ'; it is always used in the middle or at the end of a word. Examples : ৰঙা ronga) red, ৰঙিয়াল (rongiyal) cheerful, অঙহী-বঙহী (ongohi-bongohi) relatives etc.
চ (so, cho)	usually has the sound of 's' in same, side etc., as— চাবি (sabi) key, চৰকাৰ (sorkar) government, চতুৰ (sotur) clever etc., But when two 'চ' s are combined, it takes the sound of 'ch' as in charm, change, etc. example : উচ্চ (uchcho) higher, advanced.
ছ (so, chho))	is usually pronounced 's' as in ছাতি (sati)

umbrella, ছোৱালী (sowali) girl, ছবি (sobi) picture etc., but when combined with 'চ', it is pronounced as 'chh', thus :- ইচ্ছা (ichchha) willingness.

জ (jo) has the sound of 'j' in joy, judge etc.; thus— জাহাজ (jahaj) Ship, জন্ম (jonmo) birth etc.

ঝ (jho) has the combined sound of 'j' and 'h' : ঝৰ্ণা (jhorna) spring.

ঞ (ngyo, n) has the mixed nasal sound of ই + অঁ। However, it is not possible to represent this sound properly through English alphabet. The independent use of ঞ is rare. Two examples are : চিঞৰ (singyor) to scream, সিঞাৰ (xingyar) to mock. Some examples of its combined forms :

অঞ্চল (onchol) region

বুৰঞ্জী (buronji) history, বিজ্ঞান (bijnan, bigyan) science, প্ৰতিজ্ঞা (protijna, protigya). In the last two examples, only the latter forms of pronunciation are used in speech.

ট (to) has the sound of 't' in tall, toy, take, tea etc., e.g., টেঙা (taenga) sour, টান (taan) difficult, টাটকা (tatka) fresh etc.

ঠ (tho) has the combined sound of 't' and 'h', e.g., ঠিকনা (thikona) address, ঠৰঙা (thoronga) stiff, ঠাই (thai) place etc.

ড (do) is pronounced like 'd' in dog, doll, doctor, day, etc., e.g., ডাঙৰ (dangor) big, ডাল (daal) branch of a tree, ডাক (daak) mail etc.

ঢ (dho)	has the combined sound of 'd' and 'h', e.g., ঢৌ (dhou) wave, ঢেৰ (dher) a lot of, ঢেকীয়া (dhekiya) fern etc.
ণ (murdhonyo no)	pronounced like 'n' in not, nine, now e.g., কাৰণ (karon) cause, অণু (onu) atom, ৰণ (ron) battle etc.
ত (to)	is pronounced almost like English 't', but the tongue should slightly come down to touch the back of the upper front teeth, while making this sound. Examples : তৰা (tora), তলা (lock), etc.
থ (tho)	has the combined sound of 't' and 'h', and the position of the tongue should be the same as that regarding 'ত'। Examples : কথা (kotha) speech, থিয় (thiyo) standing etc.
দ (do)	is prounounced almost like the English 'd', and the tongue-position is the same as in 'ত'। Examples : দাম (daam) price, দিন (din) day, দৰব (dorob) medicine etc.
ধ (dho)	is the combination of 'd' and 'h'; and the tongue-position is the same as in 'দ'। Examples : ধান (dhan) paddy, ধূলি (dhuli) dust, etc.
ন (dontyono)	is pronounced like 'n', e.g., নাও (nao) boat, নিয়ম (niyom) rule, নদী (nodi) river, etc.
প (po)	has the sound of 'p' in poor, problem etc. Examples : পদুম (podum) lotus, পৰাজয় (porajoi) defeat, পতাকা (potaka) flag, etc.
ফ (pho)	is the combination of 'p' and 'h'; e.g., ফুল (phul) flower, ফাগুন (phagun) etc.,

ব (bo)	has the sound of 'b' : বৰণ (boron) colour, বাতৰি (batori) news, বেলেগ (baeleg) different, etc.
ভ (bho)	is the combination of 'b' and 'h' : ভাল (bhaal) good, ভয় (bhoi) fear, ভৰি (bhori) legs, etc.
ম (mo)	has the sound of 'm' as in mine, may. etc. মত (mot) opinion, মতা (mota) male, মহান (mohan) great.
য (jo), (yo)	sounds like English 'j'. There is no difference in pronunciation of 'জ' and 'য'; as, যুবতী (juboti) young woman, কাৰ্য (karjo) task etc. But 'য' maintains its original Sanskrit sound 'ya' in conjunct consonants; as— অন্যায় (onyay) unjut, ভাগ্য bhagyo) luck etc.
ৰ (ro)	has the sound of 'r' as in red, road etc., e.g., ৰন্ধা (rondha) to cook, ৰাতি (rati) night, etc.
ল (lo)	has the sound of 'l' as in light, long, etc., e.g., লতা (lota) creeper, লাভ (laabh) profit, etc.
ৱ (wo)	is pronounced like the English 'w' as in warm, towards etc., e.g., বোৱতী (bowoti) flowing (said of a river), কোৱা (kowa) say, জীৱন (jiwon) life etc.
শ (talobyoxo) ষ (murdhonyoxo) স (dontyoxo)	These three letters in Assamese are pronounced in a unique way. The sound is somewhat similar to the English 'h' as in behind, hand etc., but without any vibration of the vocal cord. In other words, while pronouncing them, initially one can hear the sound of air gushing out of the wind pipe, but the voice comes only after that.

In phonology this is called 'voiceless velar fricative'.

There is no letter in the English alphabet corresponding to this sound; however, we have used 'x' as a symbol for it.

Examples of words with these letters :

শেষ (xex) last, শত্ৰু (Xotru) enemy, শিকলি (xikoli) chain,

সৰু (xoru) small, সমান (xoman) equal; সঁচা (xonsa) true, কৃষক (krixok) farmer, ঋষি (rixi) sage, ষোল্ল (xollo) 16. However, in some words, 'স' is pronounced like 's', such as উৎস (utso) source, উৎসাহ (utsah) enthusiasm, চিকিৎসা (sikitsa) treatment etc.

But, when 'স', 'শ' and 'ষ' appear in conjunct consonants, they are pronounced like 's', 'sh', and 'sh' respectively. Examples : বিশ্লেষণ (bishlexon) analysis, পুৰস্কাৰ (puroskar) prize, কৃষ্ণ (krishno) etc.

হ (ho) — has the sound of 'h', e.g., হয়তো (hoito) perhaps, হাতী (hati) elephant, হাঁহি (hanhi) laughter.

ং onuswar) — pronounced like 'ng' as in wrong, long etc. Exmaples : ৰং (rong) colour, অংশ (ongxo) part, খং (khong) anger etc.

ঃ (bixorgo) — it is pronounced like a final breathing 'h', as— পুনঃ পুনঃ (punoh punoh) again and again, দুঃসাহস (duh xahox) dare-devilry etc.

ঁ (sondrobindu) — It gives a nasal sound to the letter on the top of which it is written, as— হাঁহ (hanh) duck, laugh; বাঁহ (banh) bamboo etc.

ক্ষ (kkha)	is a conjunct of 'ক' and 'ষ', but is pronounced like 'kkha' as প্ৰদক্ষিণ (prodokkhin) going round, ৰক্ষা (rokkha) to save, লক্ষ্য (lokkhyo) aim, etc.
ড় (ro)	during the articulation of this sound, the tip of the tongue comes close to the palate, but instead of making the sound there, it comes forward and strikes the teeth ridge with its underside; as— ঘড়ী (ghori) clock, গাড়ী (gari) car, আড়ম্বৰ (arombor) pomp and grandeur, etc.
ঢ় (rho)	is the aspirated form of ড়; examples গাঢ় (garho) deep, গঢ়োঁতা (gorhonta) maker, বাঢ় .(barh) to increase, etc.
য় (yo)	is prounced like 'y' in yoke, young, etc. examples : তেতিয়া (tetiya) then, ভয়ানক (bhoyanok) dreadful, প্ৰয়াস (proyax) effort, etc.,

Revision—Lesson

স্বৰবৰ্ণ (Vowels)

Assamese Letters	Symbols	Pronunciation
অ	o	মন, ঘৰ, অধিকাৰ, অনুমতি
আ	a, aa	কথা, পঢ়া, আম, কাম
ই	i	নিয়ম, ইয়াত
ঈ	i, ee	জীৱন, পক্ষী, গীত, বীৰ
উ	u	উট, পুখুৰী
ঊ	u, oo	উপকূল, অনুৰূপ, দূৰ, ৰূপ
ঋ	ri	হৃদয়, বৃহৎ
এ	ae, e	এক, বেৰ, এদিন, মেকুৰী
ঐ	oi	নৈতিক, ঐতিহ্য
ও	o	কোন, ওলা, পোন, ওলোটা
ঔ	ou	ঔষধ, মৌ, গৌৰৱ

(ব্যঞ্জনবৰ্ণ–Consonants)

Assamese letters	Symbols	Pronunciation
ক	k	কাম, কেনেকৈ, কৰা
খ	kh	খেল, খৰাং
গ	g	গাওঁ, গধূলি
ঘ	gh	ঘড়ী, ঘৰ
ঙ	ng	ৰঙা, অঙহী-বঙহী
চ	so, ch	চাবি, চতুৰ, উচ্চ
ছ	so, chh	ছবি, ছোৱালী ইচ্ছা
জ	j	জাহাজ, জন্ম
ঝ	jh	ঝৰ্ণা

ঞ	ngy (o)	চিঞৰ, বুৰঞ্জী, বিজ্ঞান
ট	t	টেঙা, টান, টাট্‌কা
ঠ	th	ঠিকনা, ঠৰঙা
ড	d	ঢেৰ, ঠেকীয়া
ণ	n	কাৰণ, অণু
ত	t	তৰা, তলা
থ	th	কথা, থিয়
দ	d	দাম, দিন
ধ	dh	ধান, ধূলি
ন	n	নাও, নদী
প	p	পদুম, পতাকা
ফ	ph	ফুল, ফাগুন
ব	b	বাতৰি, বেলেগ
ভ	bh	ভাল, ভয়
ম	m	মত, মহান
য	j y	যুবতী, কাৰ্য, ভাগ্য
ল	r	ৰাতি, ৰুধা
ৱ	w	জীৱন, বোৱতী
শ	x , s	শেষ, শত্ৰু, বিশ্লেষণ
ষ	x , sh	কৃষক, ঋষি, কৃষ্ণ
স	x , sh	সৰু, সমান, পুৰস্কাৰ
হ	h	হয়তো, হাতী
ং	ng	ৰং, খং, অংশ
ঃ	n	পুনঃ পুনঃ, দুঃসাহস
ঁ	–	হাঁহ, বাঁহ
ক্ষ	kkh	ৰক্ষা, লক্ষ্য
ড়	r	গাড়ী, ঘড়ী

ঢ়	ṙh	গাঢ়, গঢ়োঁতা
য়	y	তেতিয়া, ভয়ানক, প্ৰয়াস

Practice :

What is your name?

তোমাৰ নাম কি ?

(tomar naam ki?)

My name is Abhijit Bora

মোৰ নাম অভিজিত বৰা।

(Mor naam obhijit bora)

Where do you live?

তুমি ক'ত থাকা ?

(tumi kot thaka?)

I live in Delhi

মই দিল্লীত থাকোঁ।

(moi dillit thakon.)

Who are sitting there?

তাত কোন-কোন বহি আছে ?

(taat kon kon bohi ase?)

My parents are sitting there

মোৰ মা-দেউতা তাত বহি আছে।

(mor maa-dauta taat bohi ase)

Who is this girl?

এই ছোৱালীজনী কোন ?

(ei sowalijoni kon?)

She is my niece.

তাই মোৰ ভাগিন।

(toi mor bhagin)

Read and write :

বন্দে মাতৰম্
সুজলাং সুফলাং মলয়জ শীতলাং
শস্য শ্যামলাং মাতৰম্।
শুভ্ৰ-জ্যোৎস্না-পুলকিত-যামিনীম্
ফুল্লকুসুমিত-দ্ৰুমদল শোভিনীম্
সুহাসিনীং সুমধুৰভাষিণীম্
সুখদাং বৰদাং মাতৰম্।
বন্দে মাতৰম্

Bande Maataram
Sujalang Suphalang Malayajasheetalang
Shasyashamlang Maataram.
Shubhra-jyotona-pulakita yaminim
phullakusumita drumadalashobhinim,
Suhasining Sumadhurabhashinim
Sukhadang Baradang Maatarm.
Bande Maataram.

Lesson : 6

Entry Into Language

মই (moi)—I	আমি (ami)—We
তুমি (tumi)—You	তোমালোক (tomalok)—You
তই (toi)—You	তহঁত (tohont)—You
আপুনি (apuni)—You (honorific)	আপোনালোক (aponalok)—You
তেওঁ (teon)—he/she	তেওঁলোক (teonlok)—they
সি (xi)—he	সিহঁত (xihont)—they
তাই (tai)—she	তেখেতসকল (tekhetxokol)—
তেখেত (tekhet—he/she (honorific)	[they]
ল'ৰা (lora)—boy	ছোৱালী (sowali)—girl
পুতেক (putek)—son	জীয়েক (jiyek)—daughter
পুত্র (putra)—son	কন্যা (kanya)—daughter
দেউতা (dauta)—father	আই (ai)—mother
বাবা (baba) father	মা (maa) mother
ককা (koka)—grandfather	আইতা (aita)—grandmother
খুড়া (khura)—uncle (Paternal)	খুড়ী (khuri)—aunt

মই হওঁ (moi haon)—I am

আমি হওঁ (ami haon)—We are

তুমি হোৱা (tumi howa)—You are

তোমালোক হোৱা (tomalok howa)—You are

তই হব (toi howo)—You are

তহঁত হব (tohont howo)—You are

আপুনি হয় (apuni hoi)

আপোনালোক হয় (aponalok hoi)

সি হয় (xi hoi)— he is

সিহঁত হয় (xihont hoi)— they are

তেওঁ হয় (teon hoi)—he/she is

তেওঁলোক হয় (teonlok hoi)— they are'

মই কৰোঁ (moi karon)— I do

তুমি কৰা (tumi kora)— you do

আপুনি কৰে (apuni kore)— you do

তই কৰ (toi koro)— you do

তোমালোকে কৰা (tomaloke kora)— you do

আপোনালোকে কৰে (aponaloke kore)— you do

সিহঁতে কৰে (xihonte kore)—they do

অজিতে কৰে (ojite kore)—Ajit does

ইয়াত (iyat)—here, তাত (taat)—there, য'ত (jot)—where (indicative) ক'ত (kot)—where (interrogative), এইটো (eito)—this, সেইটো (xeito)—that এইবোৰ (eibor)—these, সেইবোৰ (xeibor)—those.

এই কাৰণে (ei karone)—for this, সেই কাৰণে (xei karone)—for that, কিহৰ কাৰণে (kihor karone)—for what, যাৰ কাৰণে (jar karone)—for which/for whom (indicative), কাৰ কাৰণে (kar karone)—for whom (Interrogative)

যদি (jodi)—if

কিন্তু (kintu)—but

যদিও (jodio)—though

তথাপি (tothapi)— yet, still

তাৰোপৰি (taropori)—besides

বৰং (borong)—rather

আৰু (aru)— and

বা (ba)—or

হয় (hoi)—yes

নহয় (nohoi)—no

কিয় (kiyo)—why

কাৰণ (karon)—because

যিহেতু (jihetu)—because

যেন (jaen)— as if

বাহিৰ (bahir)—out

ভিতৰ (bhitor)—in

ওপৰ (opor)—up

তল (tol)—down

ডাঙৰ (dangor)—big | সৰু (xoru)—small
বেছি (besi)—more | কম (kom)—less
যেতিয়া (jetiya)—when | এতিয়া (etiya)—now
কিমান (kiman)—how much | যিমান (jiman)—as much
ইমান (iman)—this much | সিমান (ximan)—so much

Names of the Months

বহাগ (Bohag)	জেঠ (Jeth)
আহাৰ (Ahar)	শাওন (Xaon)
ভাদ (bhado)	আহিন (Ahin)
কাতি (Kati)	আঘোণ (Aghon)
পুহ (Puh)	মাঘ (Magh)
ফাগুন (Phagun)	চ'ত (Sot)

Note : the Assamese year begins with the month of বহাগ (Bohag) i.e. from the middle of April.

Names of the Days

সোমবাৰ	(xom-bar)	Monday
মঙ্গলবাৰ	(mongol bar)	Tuesday
বুধবাৰ	(budhbar)	Wednesday
বৃহস্পতিবাৰ	(brihaspotibar)	Thursday
শুক্রবাৰ	(xukrobar)	Friday
শনিবাৰ	(xonibar)	Saturday
দেওবাৰ	(deobar)	Sunday

ছেকেণ্ড (sekend)—second মিনিট (minit)—minute ঘন্টা (ghonta)—hour, দিন (din)—day, সপ্তাহ (xaptah), পষেক (poxek)—fortnight, মাহ (maah)—month, বছৰ (bosor)—year

Names of the Seasons

গ্রীস্ম (grismo)—summar | covering বহাগ-জেঠ-আহাৰ
বৰ্ষা (borxaa)—monson | covering আহাৰ-শাওন

শৰৎ (xorot)—autumn	covering ভাদ-আহিন
হেমন্ত (hemonto)—dewyseason	covering কাতি-আঘোণ
শীত (xeet)—winter	covering আঘোণ-পুহ-মাঘ
বসন্ত boxonto)—spring	covering ফাগুন-চ'ত

Name of the directions :

পূব (poob) East	পশ্চিম (possim) West
উত্তৰ (uttar) North	দক্ষিণ (dokkhin) South
উত্তৰ-পূব (uttar-poob) North-East	দক্ষিণ-পূব (dokkhin-poob) South-East
উত্তৰ পশ্চিম (uttar-possim) North-West	দক্ষিণ-পশ্চিম (dokkhin-possim) South-West
ঊৰ্দ্ধ (oordha) Up	অধঃ (adhah) down
সোঁ (xon) Right	বাওঁ (baon) left
আগ (ag) front	পাছ (pas) back

Practice :

Amitabh is a very good boy.	অমিতাভ বৰ ভাল ল'ৰা।
Rekha is a beautiful girl.	ৰেখা এজনী ধুনীয়া ছোৱালী।
Where are they going?	তেওঁলোক ক'লৈ গৈছে ?
They are going to school.	তেওঁলোক স্কুললৈ গৈছে।
When will you go to school?	তুমি কেতিয়া স্কুললৈ যাবা ?
Today is our holiday.	আজি আমাৰ বন্ধ।
Where is your father?	তোমাৰ দেউতাৰা ক'ত ?
My father has gone to his office.	মোৰ দেউতা অফিচলৈ গৈছে।

Exercise

Translate into Assamese :—

I, boy, there, where, if, how much, this much, Friday, Monday, week, fortnight, monsoon, spring, West, East, Right, Left.

Lesson 7
Numbers
সংখ্যা

১	এক	aek	1
২	দুই	dui	2
৩	তিনি	tini	3
৪	চাৰি	sari	4
৫	পাঁচ	paans	5
৬	ছয়	soi	6
৭	সাত	xaat	7
৮	আঠ	aath	8
৯	ন	no	9
১০	দহ	doh	10
১১	এঘাৰ	aegharo	11
১২	বাৰ	baro	12
১৩	তেৰ	taero	13
১৪	চৈধ্য	soidhyo	14
১৫	পোধৰ	pondhoro	15
১৬	ষোল্ল	xollo	16
১৭	সোতৰ	xotoro	17
১৮	ওঠৰ	othoro	18
১৯	উনৈশ	unois	19
২০	বিশ	bees	20
২১	একৈশ	ekois	21
২২	বাইশ	bais	22
২৩	তেইশ	teis	23

২৪	চৌব্বিশ	soubbis	24
২৫	পঁচিশ	ponsis	25
২৬	ছাব্বিশ	sabbis	26
২৭	সাতাইশ	xatais	27
২৮	আঠাইশ	athais	28
২৯	উনত্রিশ	untris	29
৩০	ত্রিশ	tris	30
৩১	একত্রিশ	aektris	31
৩২	বত্রিশ	botris	32
৩৩	তেত্রিশ	tettris	33
৩৪	চৌত্রিশ	soùtris	34
৩৫	পঁয়ত্রিশ	pointris	35
৩৬	ছয়ত্রিশ	soitris	36
৩৭	সাতত্রিশ	xatotris	37
৩৮	আঠত্রিশ	athotris	38
৩৯	উনচল্লিশ	unsollis	39
৪০	চল্লিশ	sollis	40
৪১	একচল্লিশ	aeksollis	41
৪২	বিৰাল্লিশ	birallis	42
৪৩	তিৰাল্লিশ	tirallis	43
৪৪	চৌৰাল্লিশ	sourallis	44
৪৫	পঞ্চল্লিশ	ponchollis	45
৪৬	ছয়চল্লিশ	soisollis	46
৪৭	সাতচল্লিশ	xatsollis	47
৪৮	আঠচল্লিশ	athsollis	48
৪৯	উনপঞ্চাশ	unaponchas	49
৫০	পঞ্চাশ	ponchaas	50
৫১	একাৱন	ekawon	51

৫২	বাৱন	bawon	52
৫৩	তেম্পন	teppon	53
৫৪	চৌৱন	sowon	54
৫৫	পঁচপন	pospon	55
৫৬	ছাপ্পন	sappon	56
৫৭	সাতাৱন	xatawon	57
৫৮	আঠাৱন	athawon	58
৫৯	উনষাঠি	unoxathi	59
৬০	ষাঠি	xathi	60
৬১	এষষ্ঠি	aexosthi	61
৬২	বাষষ্ঠি	baxosthi	62
৬৩	তেষষ্ঠি	texosthi	63
৬৪	চৌষষ্ঠি	souxosthi	64
৬৫	পঁয়ষষ্ঠি	poinxoshthi	65
৬৬	ছয়ষষ্ঠি	soixosthi	66
৬৭	সাতষষ্ঠি	xatxosthi	67
৬৮	আঠষষ্ঠি	athxoshti	68
৬৯	উনসত্তৰ	unoxottor	69
৭০	সত্তৰ	xottor	70
৭১	এসত্তৰ	aexottor	71
৭২	বাসত্তৰ	baxottor	72
৭৩	তেসত্তৰ	texottor	73
৭৪	চৌসত্তৰ	souxottor	74
৭৫	পঁয়সত্তৰ	poixottor	75
৭৬	ছয়সত্তৰ	soixottor	76
৭৭	সাতসত্তৰ	xatxotton	77
৭৮	আঠসত্তৰ	athxotton	78
৭৯	উনাশী	unaaxi	79

৮০	আশী	axi	80
৮১	একাশী	ekaxi	81
৮২	বিৰাশী	biraxi	82
৮৩	তিৰাশী	tiraxi	83
৮৪	চৌৰাশী	souraxi	84
৮৫	পঁচাশী	ponsaxi	85
৮৬	ছয়াশী	soyaxi	86
৮৭	সাতাশী	xataxi	87
৮৮	আঠাশী	athaaxi	88
৮৯	উনানব্বৈ	unanobboi	89
৯০	নব্বৈ	nobboi	90
৯১	একানব্বৈ	aekanobboi	91
৯২	বিৰানব্বৈ	biranobboi	92
৯৩	তিৰানব্বৈ	tiranobboi	93
৯৪	চৌৰানব্বৈ	souranobboi	94
৯৫	পঁচানব্বৈ	ponsanobboi	95
৯৬	ছয়ানব্বৈ	soyanobboi	96
৯৭	সাতানব্বৈ	xatanobboi	97
৯৮	আঠানব্বৈ	athanobboi	98
৯৯	নিৰানব্বৈ	niranobboi	99
১০০	এশ	aexo	100
২০০	দুশ	duxo	200
৩০০	তিনিশ	tinixo	300
৪০০	চাৰিশ	sarixo	400
৫০০	পাঁচশ	pansxo	500
১০০০	এহেজাৰ	aehaezar	1000
১০,০০০	দহহাজাৰ	dohhazar	10,000
১০০,০০০	এক লাখ	aek lakh	100,000

২০০,০০০	দুই লাখ	dui lakh	200,000
১০০,০০,০০০	এক কোটি	aek koti	100,00,000

Ordinal numbers

প্ৰথম prothom) first	দ্বিতীয় (dwitiyo) second
তৃতীয় (tritiyo) third	চতুৰ্থ (soturtho) fourth
পঞ্চম (ponchom) fifth	ষষ্ঠ (xostho) sixth
সপ্তম (xoptom) seventh	অষ্টম (ostom) eighth
নৱম (nowom) ninth	দশম doxom) tenth
একাদশ (ekadox) eleventh	দ্বাদশ (dwadox) twelfth
ত্ৰয়োদশ (troyodox) thirteenth	চতুৰ্দশ (soturdox) fourteenth
পঞ্চদশ (ponchodox) fifteenth	ষোড়শ (xoroxo) sixteenth
সপ্তদশ (xoptodox) sevententh	অষ্টাদশ (ostadox) eighteenth
ঊনবিংশ (unobingxo) nineteenth	বিংশ (bingxo) twentieth

Articles

There are a number of articles in Assamese and each one of them has its specific use. A learner has to be careful while using an article, because the combination of the article ad the noun has to be appropriate.

Definite article	Indefinite article
মানুহজন (the man)	এজন মানুহ (a man)
কাগজ খিলা (the sheet of paper)	এখিলা কাগজ (a sheet of paper)
লাঠীডাল (the stick)	এডাল লাঠী (a stick)

A definite article is suffixed to the noun it refers to, while an indefinite article appears before the noun, with an এ at the beginning.

Here is a list of articles in Assamese :

a) Articles for nouns denoting human beings —

জন ঃ- (Masculine) Indicates some respect :

শিক্ষকজন (the teacher), সভাপতিজন (the president)

গৰাকী ঃ- (Both the genders) :— Indicates a high degree of respect.

অধ্যক্ষ গৰাকী (adhyokkhogoraki) the Principal, মহিলা গৰাকী (mohilagoraki) the lady.

Note : In case of women, 'গৰাকী' is also used to convey a general sense of respect.

টো - (Masculine) This doesnot indicate any respect, but a sense of intimacy is there. It may also convey a sense of contempt.

ল'ৰাটো, বন্ধুটো (the friend), মূৰ্খটো (the fool), ডকাইতটো (the robber) etc.

জনী ঃ (Feminine) Implications are same as of 'টো' । ছোৱালীজনী, বান্ধৱীজনী,

টি ঃ- (both the genders)— Indicates lovableness. ভনীটি (the younger sister), ল'ৰাটি (the boy)

Articles for other nouns :

	Definite	**Indefinitge**
টো ঃ	ঘৰটো (the house), ৰাস্তাটো (the road), কলটো (the banana)	এটা (aeta)
খন ঃ	(used with a flat object) কাঁহীখন, (the dish), পথাৰখন (the field), কিতাপখন (the book)	এখন (aekhon)
ডাল ঃ	(with a long object) লাঠী ডাল (the stick), ৰছীডাল (the rope), পেন্সিলডাল (the pencil)	এডাল (aedal)

খিলা ঃ	কাগজখিলা (the sheet of paper), পাতখিলা (the leaf)	এখিলা (ekhila)
পাত ঃ	জোতাপাত (the shoe),	এপাত (aepat)
জোপাঃ	গছজোপা (the tree), আম জোপা (the mango tree)	এজোপা (aejopa)
চটা ঃ	(with thick objects) শিলচটা (the slab of stone)	এচটা (aesota)
ডৰা ঃ	(plot of land) মাটি ডৰা, ফুলনি ডৰা (the plot where flowers have been grown)	এডৰা (aedora)

Use of articles in sentences :

ল'ৰাটো বৰ দুষ্ট The boy is very naughty.

বাতৰি কাকতখন দিয়াচোন Please give me the newspaper

এজন মানুহে আপোনাৰ কথা সুধিছে A man is asking about you.

চকীখন কোনে ভাঙিলে ? Who has broken the chair?

মই এটা নতুন ঘড়ী কিনিলো I have bought a new watch.

গছজোপা ধুমুহাত উভালি পৰিল। The tree was uprooted by the storm.

গাড়ীখন অতি পুৰণি। The car is very old.

Exercise

Translate into Assamese :

(a) 4, 10, 14, 27, 35, 45, 89, 99.

(b) Eighth, Twelfth, Seventeenth, Twenty-two, Forty-one, Sixty-nine, Eighty-four.
6th, 10th, 14th, 17th.

Lesson : 8

Nouns, Adjectives and Pronouns

বিশেষ্য, বিশেষণ আৰু সৰ্বনাম

Nouns (বিশেষ্য)

In Assamese, there are 5 (five) types of nouns :

1. Proper noun (ব্যক্তি আৰু স্হানবাচক বিশেষ্য), as— ৰাম (Ram), শ্যাম (Shyam), গুৱাহাটী (Guwahati) দিল্লী (Delhi), etc.
2. Common noun (জাতিবাচক বিশেষ্য), as— মানুহ (man), কুকুৰ (dog), চহৰ (town) etc.
3. Material noun (বস্তুবাচক বিশেষ্য) as— ঘৰ (house), বাচ (bus), গাখীৰ (milk), ঘিঁউ (ghee) etc.
4. collective noun (সমষ্টিবাচক বিশেষ্য), as—ক্লাচ (class), মেলা (fair), ভিৰ (crowd) etc. and
5. Abstract noun (গুণবাচক বিশেষ্য), as— দাৰিদ্র্য (poverty), বন্ধুত্ব (friendship), দয়া (kindness), সৰলতা (simplicity), etc.

   There are 3 (three) ways, in which abstract nouns are formed:

(a) From Common nouns, as—মানুহ (human)—মনুষ্যত্ব (humanity), বন্ধু (friend)— বন্ধুত্ব (friendship), নাৰী (woman)—নাৰীত্ব (Womanhood), etc.

(b) from adjectives, as—শ্রেষ্ঠ (superior) শ্রেষ্ঠতা (superiority), উষ্ণ (warm)— উষ্ণতা (warmth), কঠিন (hard)—; কঠিনতা (hardness), etc., and,

(c) From verbs, as—মৰা (to die)—মৃত্যু (death), শুনা (to hear)— শ্ৰৱণ (Act of hearing), etc.

Adjectives (বিশেষণ)

There are 3 (three) types of adjectives in Assamese :—

1. The adjective which qualifies a noun is 'বিশেষ্যৰ বিশেষণ,' as—
   দুষ্ট ল'ৰা (dusto lora)—naughty boy, ,
   শান্ত ছোৱালী (xanto sowali)—gentle girl, etc.
2. The adjective that qualifies another adjective is 'বিশেষণীয় বিশেষণ', as—
   বৰ ভাল ছোৱালী (bor bhaal sowali)—very good girl.
   অতি উচ্চ পদৱী (oti uchcho podobi)—very high position, etc.
3. The adjective which modifies the verb is 'ক্রিয়া বিশেষণ', as—
   লাহে লাহে খোজ কাঢ়িবা (lahe lahe khoj karhiba)—Walk slowly.
   ডাঙৰ ডাঙৰকৈ পঢ়া (dangor dangorkoi porha)—read loudly.

   In Assamese, we have 3 (three) degrees of adjectives such as Positive, Comparative and Superlative. তৰ (tar) and তম (tam) are to be added to an adjective in the positive degree to form comparative and superlative degrees respectively; as—

   বৃহৎ (brihat) large — বৃহত্তৰ (brihattar) larger and বৃহত্তম (brihattam) largest.

   দ্রুত (druta) fast — দ্রুততৰ (drutatam) faster and দ্রুততম (drutatam) fastest.

Pronouns (সর্বনাম)

মই (moi) I	আমি (ami) we
তুমি (tumi) you	তোমালোক (tomalok) you
তই (toi) you	তহঁত (tohont) you
আপুনি (apuni) you	আপোনালোক (aponalok) you
সি (xi) he	সিহঁত (xihont) they
তাই (tai) she	সিহঁত (xihont) they

তেওঁ (teon) he/she	তেওঁলোক (teonlok) they
তেখেত (tekhet) he/she	তেখেতসকল (tekhetxokol) they
যি (ji) who	যিবোৰ (ji hor) who
	যি সকল (ji xokol) who
এওঁ (eon) this	এওঁলোক (eonlok) these
এখেত (ekhet) this	এখেতসকল (ekhet xokol) these
এই (ei) this	এইবোৰ (eibor) these
	এইসকল (eixokol) these
সৌ (xou) that	সৌবোৰ (xoubor) those
কোন (kon) who	কোনবোৰ (konbor) who
কি (ki) what	কিবোৰ (ki bor) what

'আপুনি', 'তেখেত', 'এখেত', 'আপোনালোক', 'তেখেতসকল', 'এখেতসকল', 'যি সকল', 'এইসকল', তেওঁ, 'তেওঁলোক', 'এঁও', 'এওঁলোক', are used in Assamese to show respect to the perons's referred to, the degree of respect being the highest in the first eight.

Exercise

1) How many kinds of nouns and adjectives are there in Assamese? Give examples.
2) How many kinds of abstract nouns are there in Assamese? How are they formed? Give examples of each kind.
4) Translate the following words into English— মই, তাই, তেওঁলোক, তই, কোন, কি
5) Write the comparative and superlative degrees of 'বৃহৎ' and 'দ্রুত'।

Lesson : 9
Verbs
ক্ৰিয়া

মই কৰোঁ (moi koron) I do

সি কান্দে (xi kande) He cries

ল'ৰাবোৰে হাঁহে (lorabore hanhe) Boys Laugh

ছোৱালীবোৰে নাচে (Sowalibore nase) Girls dance

In the above sentences, কৰোঁ (koron), কান্দে (kande), হাঁহে (hanhe) and নাচে (nase) are the finite verbs. Verbs in Assamese do not change their forms according to their genders and numbers, as :—

The boy is coming	ল'ৰাটো আহিছে (lorato ahise)
The girl is coming	ছোৱালীজনী আহিছে (sowalijoni ahise)
The boys are coming	ল'ৰাবোৰ আহিছে (lorabor ahise)
The girls are coming	ছোৱালীবোৰ আহিছে (sowalibor ahise)

But, verbs in Assamese change their forms according to persons; ক—

I am playing	মই খেলিছোঁ (moi khelison)
We are playing	আমি খেলিছোঁ (ami khelison)
You are playing	তুমি খেলিছা (tumi khelisa)

You are playing	তোমালোকে খেলিছা (tomaloke khelisa)
You are playing	আপুনি খেলিছে (apuni khelise)
You are playing	তই খেলিছ (toi kheliso)
He is playing	তেওঁ খেলিছে (teon khelise)
She is playing	তাই খেলিছে (tai khelise)

Here is a short list of common verbs :

অহা (oha)—to come	অনা (ona)—to bring
উঠা (utha)—to rise, to get up	এৰা (aera)—to abandon
কোৱা (kowa)—to say, to speak	কঁপা (konpa)—to shiver
কটা (kota)—to cut	কাহা (kaha)—to cough
কঢ়িওৱা (korhiowa)—to carry	খোলা (khola)—to open
খোৱা (khowa) to eat	গুড়ি কৰা (guri kora)—to grind
গণনা কৰা (gonona kora)—to count	গোৱা (gowa)—to sing
ঘঁহা (ghonha)—to rub	ঘেৰা (ghera)—to surround
ঘূৰোৱা (ghurowa)—to turn	চোৱা (sowa)—to see
চলোৱা (solowa)—to drive	চিলোৱা (silowa)—to sew
চেলেকা (seleka)—to lick	চিঞৰা (singyona)—to screan
ছেকা (seka)—to filtrate	ছপোৱা (sopowa)—to print
ছটিওৱা (sotiowa)—to sprinkle	চুৰি কৰা (suri kora)—to steal
ছোৱা (sowa)—to touch	জমা কৰা (joma kora)—to save
জাগা (jaga)—to wake up	জনা (jona)—to know
জোখা (jokha)—to measure	জঁপিওৱা (jopiowa)—to jump
টনা (tona)—to pull	ঠগোৱা (thogowa)—to cheat

ডুবা (duba)—to sink

ঢলা (dhola)—to pour

থিয় হোৱা (thiyo howa)— to stand up

দিয়া (diya)—to give

দেখা (daekha)+to see

ধৰা (dhora)—to catch

নচা (nosa)—to dance

নমা (noma)—to get down

পকোৱা (pokowa)—to twist, to wind

পাহৰা (pahora)—to forget

পোৱা (powa)—to get

বগোৱা (bogowa)—to climb

বুজা (buja)—to understand

বুৰ মৰা (bur mora)— to dive

ভঙা (bhonga)—to break

মৰা (mora)—to die

যোৱা (jowa)—to go

ভবা (bhoba)—to think

লোৱা (lowa)—to take

লিখা (likha)—to write

সহ্য কৰা (xojyo kora)—to tolerate

হৰণ কৰা (horon kora)—to steal

হাঁচিওৱা (hansiowa)—to sneeze

ঢকা (dhoka)—to cover

থকা (thoka) to stay

দৌৰা (doura)—to run

দলিওৱা (doliowa)—to throw

দেখুওৱা (dekhuwa)—to show

ধোৱা (dhowa)—to wash

নিয়া (niya)—to take away

পঢ়া (porha)—to read

পঠিওৱা (pothiowa)—to send

ভঁহা (bhonha)—to float

পিটা (pita)—to beat

পোহা (poha)—to tame

বটা (bota)—to pound

বন্ধা (bondha)—to bind

বেঁকা কৰা (benka kora)—to bend

ভৰা (bhora)—to fill

মাৰা (mara)—to beat

ৰোৱা (rowa)—to wait, —to plant

লুকোৱা (lukowa)—to hide

শোৱা (xowa)—to sleep

হোৱা (howa)—to be

হত্যা কৰা (hotya kora)—to kill

হঁহা (honha)—to laugh

Participles (অসমাপিকা ক্রিয়া)

Participles are formed by adding 'ই' (i) to the main verbs; as—

কৰ্ + ই = কৰি (kori) [doing]

দেখ্ + ই = দেখি (dekhi) [seeing]

শুন্ + ই = শুনি (xuni) [hearing]

খা + ই = খাই (khai) [eating]

লিখ্ + ই = লিখি (likhi) [writing]

পা + ই = পাই pai) [getting]

Here are some examples :

1) After doing the work, have rest.
কাম কৰি জিৰণি লোৱা।
(kaam kori zironi lowa)

2) Hearing the news, I was stunned.
বাতৰিটো শুনি মই বিচূৰ্তি খালোঁ।
(Batorito xuni moi bisurti khalon)

3) Seeing you, I felt relieved.
তোমাক দেখি মই সকাহ পালোঁ।
(tomak dekhi moi xokah palon)

4) After having your meal, go to school.
ভাত খাই স্কুললৈ যোৱা।
(bhat khai skulol oi jowa)

5) Getting the prize, Munu was very happy.
পুৰস্কাৰটো পাই মুনু বৰ আনন্দিত হ'ল।
(puroskarto pai munu bor anondito hol)

Causative Verbs (পাঁচনী ক্ৰিয়া)

I have made you write a letter
মই তোমা'ৰ হতুৱাই চিঠি লিখালো
(moi tomar hotuwai sithi likhalo)

I shall make you write a poem.
মই তোমাৰ হতুৱাই / দ্বাৰা কবিতা লিখাম।

(moi tomar hotuwai/dwara kobita likham)

A list of causative verbs is given below :—

ক্ৰিয়াৰ ধাতুৰূপ	ক্ৰিয়া	পাঁচনী ক্ৰিয়া
Root of the Verb	Verb	Causative Verb
কৰ্	কৰা (to do)	কৰা, কৰোৱা (to make someone do)
ধো	ধোৱা (to wash)	ধুৱা, ধুওৱা (to make someone wash)
ল	লোৱা (to take)	লোৱা (to make someone take)
দে	দিয়া (to give)	দিয়া, দিওৱা (to make someone give)
পা	পোৱা (to get)	পোৱা (to make someone get)
শুন্	শুনা (to hear)	শুনা, শুনোৱা (to make someone hear)
খা	খোৱা (to eat)	খুৱা, খুওৱা (to make someone eat)
দেখ্	দেখা (to see)	দেখুৱা (to make someone see)
পঢ়	পঢ় (to read)	পঢ়ুৱা, পঢ়ুওৱা (to make someone teach)

Practice :—

I am eating rice.	মই ভাত খাইছোঁ (moi bhat khaison)
I am feeding you rice.	মই তোমাক ভাত খুৱাইছোঁ (moi tomak bhat khuwaison)
He writes letters.	তেওঁ চিঠি লিখে
He is making me write a letter.	তেওঁ মোৰ হতুৱাই/দ্বাৰা এখন চিঠি লিখাইছে। (Teon mor hotuwai/dwara aekhon sithi likhaise)

He is giving land to the landless cultivators.

তেওঁ ভূমিহীন কৃষকসকলক ভূমি দান কৰিছে।

(teon bhumihin krixokxokolok bhumi dan korise)

He is making somebody give land to the landless cultivators.

তেওঁ ভূমিহীন কৃষকসকলক ভূমি দান কৰোৱাইছে।

(teon bhumihin krixokxokolok bhumi dan korowaise.)

The girl drinks water.

ছোৱালীজনীয়ে পানী খায়।

(sowalijoniye pani khai)

The girl makes me drink water.

ছোৱালীজনীয়ে মোক পানী খুৱায়।

(Sowalijoniye mok pani khuwai)

: Exercise :

1) How are the participles formed in Assamese? Give three examples.

2) Give the causative forms of the following verbs :
ধোৱা, দিয়া, শুনা, কৰা, পঢ়া, পোৱা।

3) Translate into Assamese :
to do, to wash, to take, to give, to be, to get, to go, to hear, to eat, to see, to read.

Lesson : 10
TENSE
কাল
(Kal)

The word tense comes from the lating word 'tempus' (the time).

Tenses are the forms of a verb that are used to indicate the time of the action or state expressed by the verb.

There are three tenses in Assamese; They are :—

1) Present Tense : A tense that refers to an action in the present time is called the Present Tense (বৰ্তমান কাল), as— He goes to school. (তেওঁ স্কুললৈ যায়)

2) Past Tense—A tense that refers to an action in the past time is called the Past Tense (অতীত বা ভূত কাল), as—He went to school (তেওঁ স্কুললৈ গৈছিল)

3) Future Tense—A tense that refers to an action in the future time is called the Future Tense (ভবিষ্যৎ কাল), as—He will go to school (তেওঁ স্কুললৈ যাব)।

the Present Tense has four (4) forms as follows :

(a) Present Indefinite or Present Simple (নিত্য বৰ্তমান)

b) Present Continuous (স্বৰূপ বৰ্তমান)

c) Present Perfect (পুৰাঘটিত বৰ্তমান)

d) Present Perfect Continuous (নিত্যবৃত্ত বৰ্তমান)

a) The verb shows that the action is mentioned simply, without anything being said about the completeness or incompleteness of the action. Thus it is called Present Indefinite or Present Simple (নিত্য বৰ্তমান) as—I love you (মই তোমাক ভাল পাওঁ)

b) The verb shows that the action is mentioned as incomplete or continuous, that is, as still going on. It is called Present Continuous (স্বৰূপ বৰ্তমান), as—
I am reading a book (মই এখন কিতাপ পঢ়ি আছোঁ)

c) The verb shows that the action is mentioned as finished, complete at the time of speaking. It is called the Present Perfect (পুৰাঘটিত বৰ্তমান), as—
I have read the book (মই কিতাপখন পঢ়িলোঁ)

d) Here the verb shows that the action is going on continuously and not completed at the time of speaking. So it is called Present Perfect Continuous (নিত্যবৃত্ত বৰ্তমান), as—I have been reading for the last three hours (মই তিনি ঘণ্টা ধৰি পঢ়ি আছোঁ)

2. The Past Tense has 3 (three) forms in Assamese:—

(a) Past Indefinite (নিত্য ভূত/নিত্য অতীত কাল), as—
I played yesterday (মই কালি খেলিছিলোঁ)

(b) Past Continuous (ঘটমান অতীত), as—
I was playing when Rashmi arrived.
(ৰশ্মি আহি পোৱাৰ সময়ত মই খেলি আছিলোঁ)

(c) Past Perfect (পুৰাঘটিত অতীত), as—
I had done my work before you came.
(তুমি অহাৰ আগতেই মই মোৰ কাম কৰি উঠিছিলো।
The meeting had begun before I reached.

(মই গৈ পোৱাৰ আগতেই সভাখন আৰম্ভ হৈছিল)

3. Future Tense has 3 (three) forms as follows—

(a) Future Indefinite (নিত্য ভৱিষ্যৎ), as—
I shall play in the afternoon
(মই আবেলি খেলিম)

(b) Future Continuous (ঘটমান ভৱিষ্যৎ), as—
I shall be playing at 4 p.m. tomorrow.
(কাইলৈ আবেলি চাৰি বজাত মই খেলি থাকিম।)

(c) Future Perfect (পুৰাঘটিত ভৱিষ্যৎ), as—
I shall have reached there before you come.
(মই তোমাতকৈ আগতেই তাত পামগৈ)

Lesson : 11

Gender

লিঙ্গ

In Assamese, we have 4 (four) kinds of gender :—

1) পুংলিঙ্গ (punglingo) Masculine gender.
2) স্ত্ৰীলিঙ্গ (streelingo) Feminine gender.
3) উভয়লিঙ্গ (ubhoilingo) Common gender.
4) ক্লীৱলিঙ্গ (kliwolingo) Neuter gender.

Here, in the following examples, the four kinds of gender have been illustrated.

1) Masculine gender—অমিতাভ (Amitabh), ল'ৰা (boy), ককা (koka) [grandfather]
2) Feminine gender—সীতা (Sita/xita), ছোৱালী (sowali)
3) Common gender—মানৱ (manov) human being, জন্তু (jontu) animal, চৰাই (sorai) bird.
4) Neuter gender—গছ (gos) tree, গাড়ী (gari) vehicle, ঘৰ (ghor) house.

Masculine gender can be changed to feminine gender in three ways:

i) by using suffixes,
ii) by adding words of feminine denotation, and
iii) by using corresponding feminine terms.

i) (a) Feminine forms by affixing 'আ' (a)

Masculine	Feminine
মহাশয় (gentleman)	মহাশয়া

প্ৰিয়তম (dearest one)	প্ৰিয়তমা
কল্যাণীয় (lovable one)	কল্যাণীয়া

(b) Feminine forms by affixing 'ঈ' (ee)

Masculine	Faminine
মামা (Maternal uncle)	মামী (maternal aunt)
বুঢ়া (old man)	বুঢ়ী (old woman)
ছাত্ৰ (male student)	ছাত্ৰী (female student)
হৰিণ (deer)	হৰিণী (hind, doe)
ৰাক্ষস (demon)	ৰাক্ষসী (female demon)
তৰুণ (youngman)	তৰুণী (young woman)
দেৱ (god)	দেৱী (goddess)

(c) Feminine forms by affixing নী

Masculine	Feminine
বৰুৱা (Mr. Barua)	বৰুৱানী (Mrs. Barua)
গৃহস্থ (householder)	গৃহস্থনী (housewife)
চাকৰ (Man servant)	চাকৰণী (maid servant)

(d) Feminine forms by affixing 'ইনী' (ini)

Masculine	Feminine
বাঘ (tiger)	বাঘিনী (tigress)
সিংহ (lion)	সিংহিনী (lioness)
গোপ	গোপিনী

(e) Feminine forms by affixing উনী (uni)

Masculine	Feminine
ভূত (maleghost)	ভূতুনী (female ghost)
ধোবা (washerman)	ধুবুনী (washer woman)
চোৰ (male thief)	চুৰুণী (female thief)

(f) by changing the suffix 'অক' into 'ইকা'

Masculine	Feminine
নায়ক (hero)	নায়িকা (heroine)
গায়ক (male singer)	গায়িকা (female singer)
বালক (boy)	বালিকা (girl)

(ii) Feminine forms by adding words of feminine denotation—

Masculine	Feminine
মতা মানুহ (man)	তিৰোতা মানুহ (woman)
মতা কুকুৰ (dog)	মাইকী কুকুৰ (bitch)

(iii) Feminine forms by using corresponding feminine terms :—

Masculine	Feminine
শহুৰ (father-in-law)	শাহু (mother-in-law)
দৰা (bridegroom)	কইনা (bride)
দাদা (elder brother)	বাইদেউ (elder sister)
ভাই (brother)	ভনী (sister)
দেউতা (father)	মা (mother)
ল'ৰা (boy)	ছোৱালী (girl)
দেৱৰ (husband's younger brother)	ননদ (Husband's younger sister)
	জা (wife of দেৱৰ)

Exercise

1) In how many ways can masculine gender be changed into feminine gender?

2) Change the gender of the following :
শহুৰ, মতা মানুহ, গায়িকা, হৰিণ, প্ৰিয়তমা, দেৱৰ, কল্যাণীয়, মামা, বাঘ, ধোবা, ভূত, চোৰ।

Lesson : 12

Number

বচন

Like English and many other Indian languages, in Assamese also we have two numbers—

Singular (একবচন) and Plural (বহুবচন)

In Assamese, different plural suffixes are used to change the number of nouns from Singular to Plural. For nouns denoting human beings the suffixes are—

হঁত, বোৰ, বিলাক, সকল, কেইজন, কেইগৰাকী। The latter three Plural suffixes convey a sense of respect.

Here are some examples :—

Singular	**Plural**
ল'ৰা (boy)	ল'ৰা হঁত, ল'ৰাবোৰ, ল'ৰাবিলাক (boys)
মানুহ (man)	মানুহবোৰ, মানুহবিলাক, মানুহকেইজন (men)
মহিলা (lady)	মহিলাসকল, মহিলাকেইগৰাকী (ladies)
খেলুৱৈ (player)	খেলুৱৈবোৰ, খেলুৱৈসকল (players)
মূৰ্খ (fool)	মূৰ্খহঁত, মূৰ্খবোৰ, মূৰ্খবিলাক (fools)
পণ্ডিত (scholar)	পণ্ডিতসকল (scholars)

Another way of forming plurals is by adding জন, জনী, টা or গৰাকী to the specified number, thus:–

এজন ব্যক্তি (one gentleman)

পাঁচজন ব্যক্তি (five gentlemen)

তিনিগৰাকী মহিলা (three women)

দহজন পণ্ডিত (ten scholars)

সাতটা ল'ৰা (seven hoys)

Nouns, other than those denoting human bings, take the plural suffixes 'বোৰ' and 'বিলাক' to form plurals, as—

গছবোৰ (trees), বাস্তাবোৰ/ৰাস্তাবিলাক (roads), চিন্তাবোৰ (thoughts)etc.

Another way of forming plurals out of these nouns is by adding the indefinite articles to the specified numbers, as—

এজোপা গছ (one tree) তিনিজোপা গছ (three trees),

দুটা আম (two mangoes), চাৰিডাল লাঠী (four sticks) etc.

Sometimes, pluralizing words like বহুত, অনেক, ভালেমান, সকলো etc. are used with singular numbers, as—

পুতলা (toy)	বহুত পুতলা (many toys)
ছাত্ৰ (student)	সকলো ছাত্ৰ (all students)
বিদ্বান (learned person)	অনেক বিদ্বান (a number of learned persons)
মাছ (fish)	ভালেমান মাছ (plenty of fish)

Learners should, however,keep in mind that these words are not used when plural suffixes are already there. Hence, saying বহুত পুতলাবোৰ or অনেক বিদ্বানসকল will be wrong. One has to say either:

পুতলাবোৰ (toys) or বহুত পুতলা (many toys)

বিদ্বান সকল (learned persons) or অনেক বিদ্বান (many learned persons)

Plural numbers are formed by repeating the adjective also; as—

ডাঙৰ ডাঙৰ মাছ (big fish/fishes)

নতুন নতুন কিতাপ (news books)

পকা পকা আম (ripe mangoes)

Note : Fish—Collectively
একেলগে কিছু সংখ্যক মাছ
Fishes—Separate types of fish
বেলেগ বেলেগ মাছ

Practice :

ল'ৰাটোৱে হাঁহে — The boy laughs
ছোৱালীজনীয়ে কান্দে – The girl cries.
ল'ৰাবোৰে খেলে — Boys play.
ছোৱালীবোৰে নাচে — Girls dance.
মোৰ কিতাপবোৰ ক'ত ? — Where are my books?
ক'লা ক'লা কাউৰী — Black crows.
বগা বগা গৰু — White cows.

Exercise

Translate into Assamese :

Black dogs, white horses, broken mirrors, dirty lanes, old men, red birds, small fishes, ripe grapes, little boys, naughty girls.

Lesson : 13

Case

কাৰক

In Assamese, we have six kinds of cases: কৰ্ত্তা (Nominative), কৰ্ম (Objective), কৰণ (Instrumental), সম্প্ৰদান (Dative), অপাদান (Ablative), অধিকৰণ (Locative).

: Cases and their Suffixes :

Case	Suffix	Case-endings
কাৰক	বিভক্তি	বিভক্তিৰ চিন
কৰ্ত্তা	প্ৰথমা	অ, ই, এ/য়ে
কৰ্ম	দ্বিতীয়া	ক্
কৰণ	তৃতীয়া	ৰে, দি, দ্বাৰা
সম্প্ৰদান	চতুৰ্থী	ক্, লৈ
অপাদান	পঞ্চমী	পৰা
অধিকৰণ	সপ্তমী	ত্
সম্বধ	ষষ্ঠী	ৰ্

1) কৰ্ত্তা কাৰক (Nominative Case)

The nominative case specifies the one who does something, as—

কমলে কিতাপ পঢ়িছে (Kamale kitap porhise)

Kamal is reading a book.

আনন্দই খেলিছে (Anandoi khelise)

Ananda is playing.

Here, in the above mentioned two sentences কমল and আনন্দ

perform the action denoted by the verbs পঢ়িছে and খেলিছে। They are called কৰ্ত্তা (the doer).

2) কৰ্মকাৰক (Objective Case)

Whatever is done or acted upon by the verb is called কৰ্মকাৰক; as—

নবীনে অঞ্জলিক ভাল পায় (Nobine onjolik bhal pai)

Nobin loves Anjali.

খেতিয়কে মাটি চহ কৰিছে (khetiyoke mati soh korise)

The farmer is ploughing the field.

In these two sentences অঞ্জলিক and মাটি are examples of কৰ্মকাৰক (Objective case). In the second sentence the case-ending 'ক' is concealed.

In Assamese the finite verb generally comes after the object; নবীনে অঞ্জলিক ভাল পায়—here the verb 'ভাল পায়' Comes after the object 'অঞ্জলিক'; But in English the object usually comes after the verb as—My sister is writing a novel. Learners should keep in mind that while making sentences in Assamese, if the verb is placed before the object, it will be contrary to the common usage, as—খেতিয়কে চহ কৰিছে মাটি, নবীনে ভাল পায় অঞ্জলিক–such kind of composition is inappropriate. It may be used only in literary writings. Some verbs have two objects which are called দ্বিকৰ্মক (having two objects; as:

গুৰুৱে শিষ্যক বেদ পাঠ কৰাইছে

(guruwe xisyok ved path koraise)

The preceptor is teaching his disciple the Vedas.

মই তাক ভাত খুৱাইছোঁ

(moi taak bhat khuwaiso)

I am feeding him rice.

In the above mentioned sentences there are two objects: বেদ and ভাত are মুখ্য কর্ম (direct objects) and শিষ্যক and তাক are গৌণ কর্ম (indirect objects).

Note : direct object mostly relates to a thing or a subject. Indirect object is generally a person or an animal.

3) কৰণ কাৰক (Instrumental Case) কৰণ কাৰক denotes something which helps in the completion of an act; as—

কাণেৰে শুনা (karere xuna)

Hear with your ears.

হাতেৰে ভাত খোৱা (hatere bhat khowa)

Eat rice with your hand.

চোৰটো খিড়িকীয়েদি পলাই গল।

(sorto khirikiyedi polai gol)

The thief escaped through the window.

মই কল্যাণৰ যোগে তাইক খবৰটো দিয়ালো।

(moi kolyanor joge taik khoborto diyalo.)

I conveyed the message to her through Kalyan.

In the above four sentences কাঁণেৰে, হাতেৰ, খিড়িকীয়েদি and কল্যাণৰ যোগে are Instrumental cases.

4) সম্প্ৰদান কাৰক (Dative Case)

If anything is given to a person after relinquishment of giver's right, then the receiver is in the Dative case (সম্প্ৰদান কাৰক)

মাধৱে মগনীয়াক ভিক্ষা দিলে

(Madhobe mogoniyak bhikkha dile.)

Madhab gave a!ms to the beggar.

Here, মগনীয়া is in the Dative Case (সম্প্ৰদান কাৰক)।

5) অপাদান কাৰক (Ablative Case)

অপাদান কাৰক indicates something from which a thing or person is detached; as—

ডাৱৰৰ পৰা বৰষুণ পৰে

(daworor pora boroxun pore)

Rain falls from cloud.

ধূমপানৰ পৰা আঁতৰি থাকিবা।

(dhumpanor pora antori thakiba)

Abstain from smoking.

অপাদান কাৰক is generally formed by ৰ্ + পৰা

6) অধিকৰণ কাৰক (Locative Case)

অধিকৰণ কাৰক locates the time or the place, when or where, respectively, an event takes place. In Assamese, there are two kinds of অধিকৰণ কাৰক; as—

(a) কালাধিকৰণ (Locating time)

(b) আধাৰাধিকৰণ (Locating place and matter)

(a) কালাধিকৰণ ঃ

শীতকালত টাট্‌কা পাচলি পোৱা যায়।

(xeet kalot tatka pasoli powa jai)

Fresh vegetables are available in winter.

তেওঁ সপ্তাহত এবাৰকৈ আহে।

(teon xoptahot aebarkoi ahe.)

He comes once in a week.

(b) আধাৰাধিকৰণ ঃ

মই অসমত থাকোঁ।

(moi oxomot thakoni)

I live in Assam.

সাগৰৰ পানীত লোণ আছে।

(xagoror panit lon ase)

There is salt in the sea-water.

তাইৰ গানত ৰাপ আছে।

tair ganot raap ase)

She has interest in singing.

ইতিহাসত তেওঁ অদ্বিতীয়।

(itihaxot teon odwidiyo)

He in unparalleled in history.

7. সম্বন্ধ পদ (Possessive Case)

In Assamese সম্বন্ধ পদ and সম্বোধন পদ (Vocative Case) are not cases (কাৰক), because they have no direct relations with verbs in sentences, as—

মোৰ মা শুইছে (mor maa xuise)

My mother is sleeping.

তোমাৰ দাদা অফিচলৈ গৈছে।

(tomar dada ofisoloi goise)

Your brother is going to office.

In the above two sentences মোৰ and তোমাৰ have no direct relations with their verbs শুইছে and গৈছে।

8) সম্বোধন পদ (Vocative case) this is also not a case in Assamese, becuase it has no relation with the verb.

হে ভগৱান! মোক শক্তি দিয়া।

(he bhogowan! mok xokti diya)

Oh Lord! Give me strength.

বন্ধুসকল ! আমি আপোনালোকক আদৰণি জনাইছোঁ ।

(bondhuxokol! ami aponalokok adoroni jonaison)

Friends! we welcome you.

In the above two sentences হে ভগৱান and বন্ধুসকল are the examples of সম্বোধন পদ (Vocative case)

Exercise

1) How many cases are there in Assamese? Give two examples of each case.

2) Give the narration of অধিকৰণ কাৰক (Locative Case). How many kinds of অধিকৰণ কাৰক are there in Assamese? Give two examples of each.

3) Translate into Assamese.

Go outside.

Leaves fall from trees.

My brother is not at home.

Ram is greeting Hari.

This book has been sent by my uncle.

Cow eats grass.

He gave water to the thirsty.

Lesson : 14

Some Useful Sentences

কিছুমান উপযোগী বাক্য

We can convey our feelings through small phrases and sentences. Let us learn to speak briefly. Here are some phrases and short sentences.

1.	Hallo!	হেল্ল !	hallo!
2.	Happy New Year	শুভ নববৰ্ষ !	Xubho Noboborxo!
3.	Same to you.	আপোনালৈও ।	Aponalioio
4.	Happy birthday to you!	শুভ জন্মদিন !	Xubho jonomodin!
5.	Welcome to you all!	আপোনালোক সকলোকে স্বাগত জনাইছো ।	Aponalok xokoloke swagoto jonaiso.
6.	Congratulation!	অভিনন্দন !	Obhinandan!
7.	Thanks for your visit.	আপুনি অহাৰ বাবে ধন্যবাদ ।	Apuji ohar babe dhonyobad.
8.	Thank God!	ভগবান তোমাক প্ৰণাম !	Bhogoban Tomak pronam!
9.	Oh God!	হে ভগবান !	He bhogoban!
10.	Oh my darling!	হে (মোৰ) প্ৰিয়তমা !	He (mor) priyotoma!
	[to a man]	হে (মোৰ) প্ৰিয়তম !	He (mor) priyotom!

11. Bravo!	চাব্বাচ !	Sabbaas!
12. Excellent!	অপূৰ্ব !/চমৎকাৰ !	Opoorbo! Somotkaar!
13. How terrible!	কি ভয়ানক!	Ki bhoyanok!
14. How beautiful!	কি সুন্দৰ!	Ki xundor!
15. How disgraceful!	কি লজ্জাজনক !	Ki lojjajonok!
16. Absurd!	অসম্ভৱ	Oxombhov
17. Really!	সঁচা !	Xonsaa!
18. O.K.	ঠিক আছে ।	theek ase.
19. Wonderful!	অপূৰ্ব/আচৰিত!	Opoorbo!/Asorit!
20. Thank you.	ধন্যবাদ ।	Dhonyobad.
21. Certainly!	নিশ্চয় !	Nissoi!
22. What a great victory	কি মহান বিজয় !	Ki mohaan bijoi!
23. With best compliments.	শুভ কামনা সহ ! সশ্ৰদ্ধ অভিবাদন সহ	Xubho Kamona xoho. Xoshroddho Obhibadon xoho.

Some useful clauses and expressions :

1. Just a minute.	এক মিনিট ।	aek minit.
2. Just coming.	এইমাত্ৰ গৈছোঁ ।	eimatro goiso.
3. Any more?	আৰু লাগিব ?	aru lagibo?
4. Enough.	যথেষ্ট ।	jothesto.
5. Anything else?	আৰু কিবা ?	aru kiba?
6. No worry.	চিন্তা নাই ।	sinta nai.
7. As you like.	আপুনি যি ভাবে ।	apuni ji bhabe.
8. Mention not.	কোনো কথা নাই ।	kono kotha nai.

9. Nothing more	আৰু একো নালাগে।	aru aeko nalage.
10. Not at all.	একেবাৰে নহয়।	aekebare nohoi.
11. For Ladies.	মহিলাৰ বাবে।	mohilar babe.
12. To let.	ভাড়াত দিয়া হব।	bharat diya hobo.
13. No admission.	প্ৰবেশ নিষেধ।	probex nixedh.
14. No talking.	কথা পতা নিষেধ।	kotha pota nixedh.
15. No smoking.	ধূমপান নিষেধ।	dhumpan nixedh.
16. No spitting.	থু পেলোৱা নিষেধ।	thoo paelowa nixedh.

Lesson : 15

Imperative Sentences

In the following sentences, there are many verbs in the imperative mood expressing order, request or advice:—

(a) Sentences expressing order :

1.	Be quick.	লৰালৰি কৰা।	Loralori Kora.
2.	Be quiet.	মনে মনে থাকা।	Mone Mone Thaka.
3.	Come in.	ভিতৰলৈ আহা।	Bhitoroloi Aha.
4.	Get out.	ওলাই যোৱা।	Olai Jowa.
5.	Stick no bills.	বিজ্ঞাপন নলগাব।	Bigyapon nologabo.
6.	Don't talk rubbish.	বাজে কথা নক'বা।	Baje kotha nokoba
7.	Be careful.	সাৱধান হ'বা।	Xabodhan Hoba.
8.	Bring a glass of water	এগিলাচ পানী আনা।	Egilas pani ana.
9.	Don't forget to come tomorrow.	কাইলৈ আহিবলৈ নাপাহৰিবা।	Kailoi Ahiboloi napahoriba.
10.	Don't hurry.	হুৰামুৰা নকৰিবা।	Huramura nokoriba.
11.	Don't talk much.	বেছি কথা নক'বা।	Besi kotha nokoba.
12.	Speak the truth.	সঁচা কথাটো কোৱা।	Xonsa kothato kowa.
13.	Don't tell a lie.	মিছা কথা নক'বা।	Misa kotha nokoba.
14.	Go back.	উভতি যোৱা।	Ubhoti jowa.
15.	Work hard	কঠোৰ পৰিশ্ৰম কৰা।	Kathor porishrom kora.

16. Shut the window.	খিড়িকীখন বন্ধ কৰা।	Khirikikhon bondho kora.
17. Open the door.	দুৱাৰখন মেলি দিয়া।	Duwarkhon meli diya
18. Come here	ইয়ালৈ আহা। or এইফালে আহা।	Iyaloi aha. Eiphale aha.
19. Come a one	অকলে আহা।	Okole aha.
20. Sit down	বহা।	Bohaa.
21. Stand up.	থিয় হোৱা।	Thiyo howa
22. Get up early.	সোনকালে উঠিবা।	Xonkale uthiba.
23. Be ready by 7 o'clock.	সাত বজাৰ ভিতৰত সাজু হ'বা।	Xat bojar bhitorot xaju hoba.
24. Give up bad habits.	বদ অভ্যাস এৰি দিয়া।	Bod obhyax eri diya.
25. Always keep left.	সদায় বাওঁফালেদি যাবা।	Xodai baonphaledi jaba.
26. Ring the bell.	ঘণ্টা বজোৱা।	ghonta bajowa.
27. Take it away.	এইটো লৈ যোৱা।	Eito loi jowa.
28. Return the balance.	বাকী পইচা ঘূৰাই দিয়া।	Baki poisa ghurai diya.

(B) Sentences expressing request.

1. Please, excuase me.	মোক ক্ষমা কৰিব	Mok Khyoma koribo.
2. Don't mind, please.	বেয়া নাপায় যেন or, বেয়া নাপাব দেই	Beya napai jaen Beya napabo dei

	English	Assamese	Pronunciation
3.	Please, try to understnad me.	অনুগ্ৰহ কৰি মোক বুজিবলৈ চেষ্টা কৰক	Onugroh kori mok bujiboloi sesta korok.
4.	Please lend me your bicycle.	মোক আপোনাৰ চাইকেলখন দিয়কচোন	Mok aponar saikelkhon diyokson.
5.	Have some tea, please	চাহ খাওকচোন	Saah khawkson.
9.	Please deliver the goods at my residence	অনুগ্ৰহ কৰি বস্তুখিনি মোৰ ঘৰলৈ পঠাই দিব।	Onugroh kori bostukhini mor ghoroloi pothai dibo.
10.	Please, have your seat	অনুগ্ৰহ কৰি বহক।	Onugroh kori bohok.
11.	Kindly inform in time	অনুগ্ৰহ কৰি সময়মতে জনাব।	Onugroh kori xomoimote jonabo.

(C) Sentences expressing advice :

	English	Assamese	Pronunciation
1.	Let us go in time.	আমি সময়মতে যোৱা উচিত।	Ami xomoimote jowa usit.
2.	Work hard, lest you will fail	কঠোৰ পৰিশ্ৰম কৰা, নহ'লে বিফল হ'ব পাৰা	Kathor porisrom kora, nohole biphol hobo para
3.	Let us wait.	অপেক্ষা কৰা যাওক।	Opekhya kora jawk.
4.	Let us go for	ব'লা, অলপ ফুৰি	Bola, olop phuri

	a walk.	আহোঁ।	ahon.
5.	Let us make the best use of time.	সময়ৰ সদ্ব্যৱহাৰ কৰা উচিত।	Xomoyor xodbyowohar kora usit.
6.	Let it be so.	থাকক দিয়া।	Thakok diya.
7.	Let us try our best	আমি আপ্ৰাণ চেষ্টা কৰা উচিত।	Ami apran sesta kora usit.

Lesson : 16

Interrogative Sentences (1)

প্ৰশ্নবোধক বাক্য (1)

Interrogative sentences with

(a)	What	When	Where	Why	How
	কি	কেতিয়া	ক'ত	কিয়	কেনেকৈ

1.	What is your Name?	তোমাৰ নাম কি ?	Tomar Naam ki?
2.	What is your age?	তোমাৰ বয়স কিমান ?	Tomar boyox kiman?
3.	What is the time now?	এতিয়া কেই বাজিছে ?	Etiya kei bajise?
4.	What colour do you like?	তুমি কি ৰং ভাল পোৱাঁ ?	Tumi ki rong bhal powa?

No.	English	Assamese	Pronunciation
5.	When do you get up in the morning?	ৰাতিপুৱা আপুনি কিমান পৰত উঠে ?	Ratipuwa apuni kiman porot uthe?
6.	When did you hear the news?	খবৰটো আপুনি কেতিয়া শুনিলে ?	Khoborto apuni ketiya xunile?
7.	Where are you going?	তুমি ক'লৈ যোৱা ?	Tumi koloi jowa?
8.	Where does this path lead to?	এই ৰাস্তাটো ক'লৈকে আছে ?	Ei rastato koloike ase?
9.	Where have you come from?	আপুনি ক'ৰ পৰা আহিছে ?	Apuni kor pora Ahise?
10.	Why don't you come early?	তুমি সোনকালে কিয় নাহা ?	Tumi xonkale kiyo naha?
11.	Why don't you answer my queries?	তুমি মোৰ প্ৰশ্নৰ উত্তৰ নিদিয়া কিয় ?	Tumi mor prosnor uttor nidiya kiyo?
12.	How did you know that I was here?	মই ইয়াত আছো বুলি তুমি কেনেকৈ জানিলা ?	Moi iyat aso buli tumi kenekoi janila?
13.	How can I help you?	মই আপোনাক কেনেদৰে সহায় কৰিব পাৰোঁ ?	Moi aponak kenedore xohai koribo paron?
(b)	Who	Whom	Whose
15.	Who is that man?	সেই মানুহজন কোন ?	Xeimahuhjon kon?

16.	Who sang this song?	এই গানটো কোনে গাইছে ?	Ei ganto kone gaise?
17.	whom do you want to see?	আপুনি কাক লগ পাব বিচাৰিছে ?	Apuji kaak log palo bisarise?
18.	Whom are you waiting for?	আপুনি কালৈ বাট চাই আছে ?	Apuni kaaloi bat sai ase?
19.	To whom are you writng?	আপুনি কালৈ লিখিছে ?	Apuni kaaloi likhise?
20.	Whose book is this?	এইখন কাৰ কিতাপ ?	Eikhon kaar kitap?
21.	Whose name is Anil?	অনিল কাৰ নাম ?	Anil kaar naam?

Lesson : 17

Interrogative Sentences (2)

প্ৰশ্নবোধক বাক্য (2)

Interrogative sentences with

(a) IS ARE AM WAS WERE

1.	Is Assamese difficult?	অসমীয়া ভাষা টান নেকি ?	Oxomiya bhaxa taan neki?
2.	Is your name Rajiv?	তোমাৰ নাম ৰাজীৱ নেকি ?	Tomar naam Rajiv neki?

3.	Are you feeling unwell?	আপোনাৰ গা বেয়া লাগিছে নেকি ?	Aponar gaa beya lagise neki?
4.	Are you afraid of ghosts?	তোমাৰ ভূতলৈ ভয় লাগে নেকি ?	tomar bhutoloi bhoi lage neki?
5.	Am I to answer you?	কি, মই তোমাক উত্তৰ দিব লাগিব নেকি ?	Ki, moi tomak uttor dibo lagibo neki?
6.	Am I your servant?	মই তোমাৰ চাকৰ নেকি ?	Moi tomar sakor neki?
7.	Was he your friend?	তেওঁ তোমাৰ বন্ধু আছিল নেকি ?	Teon tomar bondu asil neki?
8.	Was she frightened?	তেওঁ ভয় খাইছিল নেকি ?	Teon bhoi khaisil neki?
9.	Were you tired after you returned?	ঘূৰি অহাৰ পাছত তুমি ভাগৰি পৰিছিলা নেকি ?	Ghuri ohar pasot tumi bhagori porisila neiki?
		ঘূৰি অহাৰ পাছত আপুনি ভাগৰি পৰিছিল নেকি ?	ghuri ohar pasot apuni bhagori porisil neki?

(b) DO DOES DID

10.	Do I talk too much?	মই বৰ বেছি কথা কওঁ নেকি ?	Moi bor besi kotha kawn neki?
11.	Do you smoke?	আপুনি ধূমপান কৰে নেকি ?	Apuni dhumpan kore neki?
12.	Does he come every Sunday?	তেওঁ প্ৰতি দেওবাৰে আহে নেকি ?	Teon proti deobare ahe neki?

13.	Does he like his neighbours?	তেওঁ তেওঁৰ ওচৰ চুবুৰীয়াক ভাল পায় নে ?	Teon teonr osor suburiyak bhal paine?
14.	Did you know that I would come?	মই আহিম বুলি তুমি জানিছিলানে ?	Moi ahim buli tumi janisilane?
15.	Did you ring the bell?	তুমি বে'ল বজাই-ছিলা নেকি ?	Tumi bell bojaisila neki?
(c)	HAVE HAS HAD		
16.	Have you ever driven a car?	তুমি কেতিয়াবা গাড়ী চলাইছানে ?	Tumi ketiaba gari solaisane?
17.	Have you found my handkerchief?	তুমি মোৰ ৰুমালখন পালানে ?	Tumi mor rumalkhon palane?
18.	Has her temperature gone down?	তাইৰ জ্বৰ এৰিছেনে ?	Tair jor erisene?
19.	Has Raju taken his medicine?	ৰাজুৱে দৰব খালেনে ?	Rajuwe dorob khalene?
20.	Had the postman deliver any letter?	পিয়নে কিবা চিঠি দিছিল নেকি ?	Piyone kiba sithi disil neki?
21.	Had you read it before?	তুমি এইটো আগতে পঢ়িছিলা নেকি ?	Tumi eito agote porhisila neki?

Lesson : 18

Interrogative Sentences

প্ৰশ্নবোধক বাক্য (3)

Interrogative sentences with :

(a)	How	How Long	How many	How much
	কেনেকৈ/	কিমান সময়	কিমান	কিমান
	কেনেদৰে/	কিমান পৰ	কেইটা	
	কেনে	কিমান দিন		

1.	How are you?	আপুনি কেনে আছে ? or, আপোনাৰ ভালনে ?	Apuni kene ase? Aponar bhalne?
2.	How did you know that I was here?	মই ইয়াত আছোঁ বুলি তুমি কেনেকৈ জানিলা ?	Moi iyat aso buli tumikenekoi janila
3.	How long have you been in Guwahati?	আপুনি গুৱাহাটীত কিমান দিন ধৰি আছে ?	Apuni Guwahatit kiman din dhori ase?
4.	How long has your mother been sick?	তোমাৰ মা কেতিয়াৰ পৰা অসুস্থ হৈ আছে ?	Tomar Maa ketiyar pora Oxustho hoi ase?
5.	How many family members do you have?	তোমালোকৰ পৰিয়ালৰ সদস্য কেইজন ?	Tomalokor poriyalor xodosyo keijon?
6.	How many seats are there in the	বাছখনত কিমান চিট আছে ?	Bas khonot kiman seat ase?

	bus?		
7.	How much money is to be paid?	কিমান টকা দিব লাগিব ?	Kiman toka dibo lagibo?
8.	How much milk is required?	কিমান গাখীৰ লাগিব ?	Kiman gakhir lagibo?
	or	কিমান গাখীৰৰ আৱশ্যক ?	Kiman gakhiror awoshyok?

Lesson : 19

Negative Sentences

নঞাৰ্থক বাক্য

Negative sentences with :

1.	My father is not feeling well.	মোৰ দেউতাৰ গা ভাল নহয়।	Mor deutar goa bhal nohoi.
2.	We are not fools.	আমি মূৰ্খ নহওঁ।	Ami, murkho nohown.
3.	I donot know him.	মই তেওঁক চিনি নাপাওঁ।	Moi teonk sini napaon.
4.	I do not understand.	মই বুজি পোৱা নাই।	Moi buji powa nai.
5.	I know nothing about it.	মই এই বিষয়ে একো নাজানো	Moi ei bixoye aeko najano.
6.	I did not want anything.	মই একো বিচৰা নাছিলো।	Moi eko bisora nasilo.

7. No throughfare.	অহা যোৱা কৰা নিষেধ।	Oha jowa kora nixedh.
8. No, not at all, He is not trustworthy.	নাই, একেবাৰেই নহয়, তেওঁ বিশ্বাসযোগ্য নহয়।	Nai, aekebarei nohoi, Teon bishwax jogyo nohoi.
9. I have never seen such a difficult man.	মই এনেকুৱা অবুজ মানুহ কাহানিও দেখা নাই।	Moi enekua obuj manuh kahanjo dekha nai.
10. She seldom smiles.	তাই কেতিয়াবাহে হাঁহে।	Tai ketiyabahe hanhe.
11. Do not touch it.	ইয়াত হাত নিদিব। or এইটো নুছুব।	Iyat hat nidibo. Eito nusubo.

B) Negative Interrogative Sentences

নঞৰ্থক প্ৰশ্নবোধক বাক্য ঃ

12. Weren't you aware of the fact?	তুমি আচল কথাটো জনা নাছিলা জানো ?	Tumi asol kothato jona nasila jano?
13. Won't that milk be enough?	সেইখিনি গাখীৰেই যথেষ্ট নহ'বনে ?	Xeikhi gakhirei jotheshto nohobone?
14. Isn't it time to close the shop?	দোকান বন্ধ কৰিবৰ হোৱা নাই জানো ?	Dokan bondho koribor howa nai jano?
15. Can't you ask him to leave?	তুমি তাক গুচি যাবলৈ ক'ব নোৱাৰানে ?	Tumi tak gusi jaboloi kobo nowarane?
16. Shouldn't you get	তুমি এতিয়া সাজু হ'ব	Tumi etiya xazu

ready now?	নালাগে জানো ?	hobo nalage jano?
17. Aren't we going for a walk now?	আমি এতিয়া ফুৰিব-লৈ নাযাম জানো ?	Ami etia phuriboloi najam jano?

Lesson : 20

Proverbs & Idioms

পটন্তৰ আৰু জতুৱা ঠাঁচ

1. All is well that ends well. — শেষ ভালেই সকলো ভাল। (xex bhalei xokolo bhal)
2. A friend in need is a friend indeed. — বিপদৰ বন্ধুৱেই আচল বন্ধু। (bipodor bondhuei asol bondhu)
3. All that glitters is not gold. — জকমকীয়া মাত্রেই সোণ নহয়। (jokmokia matrei xon nohoi)
4. As you sow, so you reap. — যেনে কাম, তেনে ফল। (jene kaam, tene phol)
5. A burnt child dreads the fire. — এবাৰ সাপে খালে লেজুলৈকো ভয়। (aebar xape khale lezuloiko bhoi)
6. Carrying coals to New Castle. — তেলীৰ মূৰত তেল। (telir murot tael)
7. Empty vessel sounds much. — ঢোৰা সাপৰ ফোঁচফোঁচনিয়েই সাৰ।

	(dhora xapor phonsphosoniei xaar)
8. Examples are better than precepts.	উপদেশতকৈ আৰ্হি ভাল। (upodexotkoi aarhi bhal)
9. Cut your coat according to your cloth.	আয় চাই ব্যয় কৰিবা। (ali sai byoi koriba)
10. No pain, no gain.	দুখ নকৰিলে মুখ নভৰে। (dukh nokorile mukh nobhore)
11. Health is wealth.	স্বাস্থ্যই পৰম ধন। (swasthyoi porom dhon)
12. Honesty is the best policy.	সততাই শ্ৰেষ্ঠপথ। (xototai srestho poth)
13. Look before you leap.	নেচাই ডেলে গালৈকে ঘাটি। (nesai dele gaaloike ghati)
14. You can take the horse into water, but you cannot make him drink.	অবুজনক বুজোৱা, ঢেৰুৱা ঠাৰি সিজোৱা। (obujonok bujowa, dheruwa thari xijowa)
15. Half a loaf is better than no loaf.	নাই মোমাইতকৈ কণা মোমায়েই ভাল। (nai momaitkoi kona momayei bhal)
16. Rome was not built in a day.	ভুকুতে কল নপকে। (bhukute kol nopoke)
17. Tit for tat.	যেন কুকুৰ, তেন টাঙোন। (jaen kukur, taen tangon)

Idioms :

1. At one's beck and call.	আঙুলিৰ মূৰত নচুবা।

		(angulir murot nosuwa)
	He is at his wife's beck and call.	তাক ঘৈণীয়েকে আঙুলিৰ মূৰত নচুৱায়। (tak ghoiniyeke angulir murot nosuwai)
2.	Fits and starts.	এৰা-ধৰাকৈ। (aera dhorakoi)
	You will fail, if you work by fits and starts.	এৰা-ধৰাকৈ কাম কৰিলে তুমি বিফল হ'বা। (aera-dhorakoi kam korile tumi biphol hoba)
3.	Hard and fast	ধৰা-বন্ধা।
	There is no hard and fast way to success.	সফলতাৰ কোনো ধৰা-বন্ধা পথ নাই। (xopholotar kono dhora-bondha poth nai)
4.	Bag and baggage.	টোপোলা টাপলিৰে সৈতে (topola tapolire xoite)
	Nobin had to leave the place bag and baggage.	নবীনে টোপোলা টাপলিৰে সৈতে ঠাইডোখৰ এৰিবলগা হ'ল। (nobine topola tapolire xoite thaidokhor eribologa hol)
5.	Part and parcel.	অবিচ্ছেদ্য অংগ। (obichchhedyo ongo)
	Kashmir is part and parcel of India.	কাশ্মীৰ ভাৰতৰ অবিচ্ছেদ্য অংগ। (kashmir bharotor obichchhedyo ongo)

6.	At sixes and sevens	খেলি-মেলি।
		(kheli meli)
	After entering my room.	মোৰ কোঠাত সোমাই দেখিলোঁ
	I found my things at	মোৰ গোটেইবোৰ বস্তু খেলি-মেলি
	sixes and sevens.	হৈ আছে।
		(mor kothat xomai dekhilo
		mor goteibor bostu kheli
		meli hoi ase.)
7.	Then and there	তৎক্ষণাত or, তেতিয়াই
		(totkhyonat)
	I took one look at the car,	মই গাড়ীখনত এবাৰ চকু
	and offered to buyit then	ফুৰালোঁ, আৰু তেতিয়াই কিনিম
	and there.	বুলি ক'লো।
		(moi garikhonot aebar soku
		phuralo aru tetiyai
		kinim buli kolo)
8.	By hook or by crook.	যি কোনো প্ৰকাৰে।
		(ji kono prokare)
	You have to do this job	যি কোনো প্ৰকাৰে তুমি এই
	by hook or by crook.	কামটো কৰিব লাগিব।
		(ji kono prokare tumi ei
		kamto koribo lagibo)
9.	Safe and sound.	ভালে-কুশলে
		(bhale-kuxole)
	She reached home safe	তাই ভালে-কুশলে ঘৰ পালেগৈ।
	and sound.	(tai bhale kuxole ghor palegoi)
10.	Null an void	বাতিল
		(batil)

The court has declared that rule will and void.	আদালতে সেই নিয়মটো বাতিল কৰিছে। (adalote xei niyomto batil korise.)
11. Out and out	সম্পূৰ্ণৰূপে (xompurnorupe)
The man was out and out a cheat.	মানুহটো সম্পূৰ্ণৰূপে এটা ঠগ আছিল। (mahuhto xompurno rupe aeta thog asil)
12. Through and through.	সম্পূৰ্ণৰূপে (Xompurnorupe)
The man is honest through and through.	মানুহজন সম্পূৰ্ণৰূপে সৎ। (mahuhjon Xompurnorupe xot)
13. One by one	এজন এজনকৈ।
Come one by one and take your prizes.	এজন এজনকৈ আহি নিজৰ নিজৰ পুৰস্কাৰ লোৱাহি। (aejon aejonkoi ahi nijor nijor puroskar lowahi)
14. Rhyme or reason	কাৰণ (karon)
He was beaten without any rhyme or reason.	সি বিনা কাৰণতে মাৰ খালে। (xi bina karonote maar khale)
15. Sooner or later.	এদিন নহয় এদিন। (edin nohoi edin)
Sooner or later he will agree with me.	এদিন নহয় এদিন তেওঁ মোৰ সৈতে একমত হ'বই। (edin nohoi edin teonmor

xoite aekmot hoboi)

16. Ins and outs. — পুংখানুপুংখ
(punkhanupunkho)

I know the ins and outs of the matter. — মই বিষয়টোৰ পুংখানুপুংখ জানো।
(moi bixoitor punkhanu punkho jano)

17. Off and on — মাজে-সময়ে

He comes to me off and on. — তেওঁ মাজে সময়ে মোৰ ওচৰলৈ আহে।
(teon maje-xomoye mor osoroloi ahe)

18. A man of word — এক কথাৰ মানুহ।

Sohoria is a man of word. — চহৰীয়া এক কথাৰ মানুহ।
(sohoriya aek kothar manuh)

19. A dead letter. — অপ্রচলিত
(oprosolito)

That rule is now a dead letter. — নিয়মটো এতিয়া অপ্রচলিত হৈ পৰিল।
(niyomto etiya aprosolito hoi poril)

20. Live from hand-to-mouth. — পেটে-ভাতে খোৱা
(paete bhate khowa)

Many people in India live from hand-to-month. — ভাৰতবৰ্ষৰ বহুত মানুহেই পেটে-ভাতে খাই আছে।
(bharot boroxor bohut manuhei paete-bhate

	khai ase)
21. Caughtred handed	হাতে লোতৰে ধৰা পৰা।
The thief was caught red-handed	চোৰটো হাতে লোতৰে ধৰা পৰিল।
	(sorto hate-lotore dhora poril)
22. A stone's throw.	ৰিং মাৰিলে শুনা।
	(ring marilei xuna)
My house is a stone's throw from the station.	মোৰ ঘৰটো ষ্টেচনৰ পৰা ৰিং মাৰিলেই শুনা দূৰত।
	(mor ghorto stesonor pora ring marilei xuna durot.)
23. To leave no stone unturned.	সকলো প্ৰকাৰে চেষ্টা কৰা।
He left no stone unturned to get a job.	তেওঁ চাকৰি এটাৰ কাৰণে সকলো প্ৰকাৰে চেষ্টা কৰিলে।
	(teon sakori aetar karone xokoloprokare sesta korile)
24. Wide of the mark.	অপ্ৰাসঙ্গিক।
Your remark is wideof the mark	তোমাৰ মন্তব্য অপ্ৰাসঙ্গিক।
	(tomar montobyo opraxongik).
25. Ups and downs.	উত্থান-পতন।
	(utthan-poton)
I have seen many ups and downs in life.	মই জীৱনত বহু উত্থান পতন দেখিছোঁ।
	(moi jiwonot bohu utthanpoton dekhiso)

Lesson : 21
Assamese Conversation
1. Father and Daughter
দেউতাক আৰু জীয়েক
(deutak aru jiyek)

Daughter :	Good morning papa, here is your bed tea.	জীয়েক ঃ	গুড মৰ্ণিং দেউতা, এয়া চাহ খাওক। (good morning deuta, eya saah khawk.)
Father :	Good morning child, What is the time?	দেউতাক ঃ	গুড মৰ্ণিং মাজনী। এতিয়া কেই বাজিছে ? (good morning maajoni. Etiya kei bajise?
Daughter :	It is seven o'clock.	জীয়েক ঃ	এতিয়া সাত বাজিছে। (etiya xat bajise)
Father :	Please get me the newspaper.	দেউতাক ঃ	মোক বাতৰি কাকতখন দিয়াচোন। (mok batori kakotkhon diyason)
Daughter :	I will just get it.	জীয়েক ঃ	এইমাত্ৰ আনিছোঁ। (ei matro aniso)
Father :	The tea is quite good, who has prepared it?	দেউতাক ঃ	চাহকাপ বঢ়িয়া হৈছে, কোনে বনাইছে ?

			(sahkap borhiya hoise, kone bonaise?
Daughter :	Mother has prepared it.	জীয়েক ঃ	মাই বনাইছে। (maai bonaise)
Father :	Where is your mother?	দেউতাক ঃ	তোমাৰ মা ক'ত ? (tomar maa kot?)
Daughter :	She is preparing breakfast in the kitchen.	জীয়েক ঃ	মাই পাকঘৰত পুৱাৰ জলপান তৈয়াৰ কৰিছে। (maai pakghorot puwar jolpan toiar korise)
Father :	What is the special dish today?	দেউতাক ঃ	আজি ভাল বস্তু কি আছে ? (aji bhal bostu ki ase?)
Daughter :	Parathas and carrot halwa.	জীয়েক ঃ	পৰঠা আৰু গাজৰৰ হালুৱা। (porotha aru gajoror haluwa)
Father :	Oh! these are my favourite dishes.	দেউতাক ঃ	আঃ ! দুয়োটাই মোৰ প্ৰিয় বস্তু। (ah! duyotai mor priyo bostu)
Daughter :	That is why she has made them today.	জীয়েক ঃ	সেই কাৰণেই মাই আজি এই দুবিধ বস্তু বনাইছে। (xei karonei maai aji

			ei dubidh bostu bonaise)
Father :	Then I shall get ready soon.	দেউতাক ঃ	তেনেহ'লে মই লৰালৰিকৈ সাজু হওঁ গৈ। (teneholemoi loralorikoi xaju howngoi)
Daughter :	Do you remember your promise?	জীয়েক ঃ	আপুনি কি কথা দিছিলে, মনত আছে তো ? (Apuni ki kotha disile, monot ase to?)
Father :	What promise?	দেউতাক ঃ	কি কথা দিছিলোনো ? (ki kotha disilono?)
Daughter :	Today is a holiday. So you have to take us all to the zoo.	জীয়েক ঃ	আজি বন্ধৰ দিন। গতিকে আপুনি আজি আমাক আটাইকে চিৰিয়াখানা দেখুৱাবলৈ নিব বুলি কৈছিল। (aji bondhor din, gotike apuni aji amak ataike siriyakhana dekhuaboloi nibo buli koisil.)
Father :	No dear, I am busy today.	দেউতাক ঃ	নহয় মাজনী, আজি মই ব্যস্ত। (nohoi maajoni, aji moi byosto.)

Daughter :	But Daddy, I have invited my friends.	জীয়েক ঃ	কিন্তু দেউতা, মই মোৰ বন্ধুবোৰক তো মাতি থৈছো। (kintu deuta, moi mor bondhu borok to mati thoiso)
Father :	At what time will they come?	দেউতাক ঃ	তেওঁলোক কিমান সময়ত আহিব ? (teonlok kiman xomoyat ahibo?)
Daughter :	I have called them at 11 a.m.	জীয়েক ঃ	মই তেওঁলোকক ১১ বজাত মাতিছোঁ। (moi teonlokok egharo bojat matiso)
Father :	All right, I will try to finish my work by then.	দেউতাক ঃ	ঠিক আছে, মই ১১ বজাৰ ভিতৰত মোৰ কাম শেষ কৰিবলৈ চেষ্টা কৰিম। (thik ase, moi egharo bojar bhitorot mor kam xex koriboloi sesta korim.)
Daughter :	Thank you very much papa! You are always very nice!	জীয়েক ঃ	ধন্যবাদ দেউতা। আপুনি আপুনি ইমান ভাল। (dhonyobad deuta! apuni imaan bhal!)
Father :	Have you spoken	দেউতাক ঃ	তুমি তোমাৰ মাৰ

	to your mother regarding today's programme?		মাৰ লগত এই বিষয়ে কথা পাতিছানে ? (tumi tomar maar logot ei bixoye kotha patisane?
Daughter :	Yes papa, She is also coming with us.	জীয়েক ঃ	হয় দেউতা। মাও আমাৰ আমাৰ লগত যাব। (hoi deuta. maao amar logot jabo)
Father :	Then go and make arrangements for the picnic.	দেউতাক ঃ	তেন্তে যোৱা, পিকনিকৰ কাৰণে আয়োজন কৰাগৈ। (Tente jowa, piknikor karone ayojon koragoi)
Daughter :	O.K. papa, I shall go. Give me the cup.	জীয়েক ঃ	ঠিক আছে দেউতা, মই যাওঁ। কাপটো দিয়ক। (Thik ase deuta, moi jaon. Kap to diyok.)

2. MOTHER AND SON
মাক আৰু পুতেক
(maak aru putek)

Mother :	You are back from your office?	মাক ঃ	অফিচৰ পৰা আহিলা ? (Ofisor pora ahila?)
Son :	Yes, mummy, but I am very tired today.	পুতেক ঃ	অঁ মা। কিন্তু আজি বৰ ভাগৰি পৰিছো। (On maa. kintu aji bor bhagori poriso.)
Mother :	Was there a lot of work today?	মাক ঃ	আজি বহুত কাম আছিল নেকি ? (Aji bohut kam asil neki?)
Son :	Yes, I was quite busy.	পুতেক ঃ	অঁ, মই বৰ ব্যস্ত হৈ আছিলো। (On, moi bor byosto hoi asilo.)
Mother :	Go and wash yourself. In the meantime I am preparing your tiffin.	মাক ঃ	যোৱা, হাত মুখ ধুই লোৱা। মই তোমাৰ কাৰণে জলপান তৈয়াৰ কৰোঁ। (Jowa, hat-mukh dhui lowa. Moi tomar karone jolpan toiar koro)

Son :	I am going. In the meantirne you prepare my tea.	পুতেক ঃ	মই গৈছো। তুমি মোৰ কাৰণে চাহ কৰাচোন। (Moi goiso. tumi mor karone sah korason)
Mother :	What would you like to have with tea?	মাক ঃ	চাহৰ লগত কি খাবা ? (Sahor logot ki khaba)
Son :	I am quite hungry Get me something heavy to eat.	পুতেক ঃ	মোৰ খুব ভোক লাগিছে। অলপ গধুৰ বস্তু খাম। (Mor khoob bhok lagise. Olop godhur bostu kham.)
Mother :	Shall I make chow-min?	মাক ঃ	চাউ-মিন বনাই দিওঁ নেকি ? (Chow-min bonai diwn neki?)
Son :	Yes, but hurry up.	পুতেক ঃ	দিয়া, কিন্তু লৰা লৰিকৈ। (Diya, kintu lora lorikoi)
Mother :	Would you like to change?	মাক ঃ	কাপোৰ সলাই ল'বা নেকি ? (Kapor xolai loba neki?)
Son :	No, I have to go again after taking tea.	পুতেক ঃ	নাই, নসলাওঁ, চাহ খায়েই মই আকৌ যাব লাগিব। (Nai, noxolawn, sah

			khayei moi akou jab lagibo.)
Mother :	Will yoiu be late?	মাক ঃ	ঘূৰি আহোঁতে দেৰি হ'ব নেকি ? (Ghuri ahonte deri hobo nei?)
Son :	I will come back by dinner.	পুতেক ঃ	ৰাতি ভাত খোৱাৰ সময়লৈ পামহি। (Rati bhat khowar xomoyoloi paamhi)
Mother :	O.K. I am goint to make Tea.	মাক ঃ	ঠিক আছে, মই চাহ কৰোঁ গৈ। (Thik ase, moi sah koron goi)
Son :	Debajit will also dine with us tonight.	পুতেক ঃ	দেবজিতেও আজি ৰাতি আমাৰ লগত ভাত খাব। (Debajiteo aji rati amar logot bhat khabo.)
Mother :	Have you invited him?	মাক ঃ	তুমি তেওঁক ভাত খাবলৈ মাতিছা নেকি ? (Tumi teonk bhat khaboloi matisa neiki?
Son :	Yes, he is alone in his house today.	পুতেক ঃ	অঁ, তেওঁৰ ঘৰত আজি কোনো নাই। (On, teonr ghorot aji

kono nai)

Mother : Then surely bring him with you.
মাক ঃ তেতিয়া হ'লে তেওঁক জৰুল লৈ আহিবা।
(Tetiyahole teonk jorul loi ahiba.)

Son : O.K.; I am going now.
পুতেক ঃ ঠিক আছে, মই যাওঁ।
(Thik ase, moi jaon.)

Mother : Come in tirne.
মাক ঃ সময়মতে আহিবা।
(Xomoimote ahiba)
or, সোনকালে আহিবা।
(Xon kale ahiba)

3. TALKING TO A GIRL

এজনী ছোৱালীৰ লগত কথা-বতৰা

(aejoni sowalir logot kotha-botora)

Q. What is your narne?
প্ৰশ্ন ঃ তোমাৰ নাম কি ?
(Tomar naam ki?)

A. My name is Nilima Hazarika.
উত্তৰ ঃ মোৰ নাম নীলিমা হাজৰিকা।
(Mor naam nilima hazorika)

Q. Where do you live?
প্ৰশ্ন ঃ তুমি ক'ত থাকা ?
(Tumi kot thaka?)

A. I live in Dibrugarh.
উত্তৰ ঃ মই ডিব্ৰুগড়ত থাকোঁ।
(Moi dibrugorot thakon)

Q. How old are you?	প্ৰশ্ন ঃ তোমাৰ বয়স কিমান ? (Tomar boyox kiman?)
A. I am Fourteen years old.	উত্তৰ ঃ মোৰ বয়স চৈধ্য বছৰ। (Mor boyox soidhyo bosor)
Q. In which class are you?	প্ৰশ্ন ঃ তুমি কোন শ্ৰেণীত পঢ়া ? (Tumi kon srenit porha?)
A. I am in class Nine.	উত্তৰ ঃ মই নৱম শ্ৰেণীত পঢ়ো। (Moi nowom srenit porho)
Q. Who else do you have in your family?	প্ৰশ্ন ঃ তোমাৰ পৰিয়ালত আৰু কোন কোন আছে ? (Tomar poriyalot aru kon kon ase?
A. Father, mother and one brother.	উত্তৰ ঃ দেউতা, মা আৰু এজন দাদা। (deuta, maa aru aejon dada.)
Q. What is your father?	প্ৰশ্ন ঃ তোমাৰ দেউতাৰাই কি কৰে ? (Tomar deutarai ki kore?)
A. Heis a teacher.	উত্তৰ ঃ তেওঁ এজন শিক্ষক। (Teon aejon xikhyok.)
Q. Does your mother also work?	প্ৰশ্ন ঃ তোমাৰ মায়েৰাইও কাম কৰে নেকি ? (Tomar mayeraio kam kore neki?)
A. No, she is a housewife.	উত্তৰ ঃ নকৰে। তেওঁ এগৰাকী গৃহিণী। (Nokore. Teon aegoraki

		grihini.)
Q. How old is your brother?	প্ৰশ্ন ঃ	তোমাৰ দাদাৰ বয়স কিমান ? (Tomar dadar boyox kiman?)
A. He is fifteen year old.	উত্তৰ ঃ	তেওঁৰ বয়স পোধৰ বছৰ । (Teonr boyox pondhoro bosor.)
Q. What would you like to become when you grow up?	প্ৰশ্ন ঃ	তুমি ডাঙৰ হ'লে কি হ'ব বিচাৰা ? (Tumi dangor hole ki hobo bisara?)
A. I would like to become a doctor.	উত্তৰ ঃ	মই ডাক্তৰ হ'ব বিচাৰো । (Moi daktor hobo bisaro)
Q. Any special reason for this choice?	প্ৰশ্ন ঃ	তুমি এই পথ বেছি লোৱাৰ কিবা বিশেষ কাৰণ আছে নেকি ? (Tumi ei poth basi lowar kiba bixex karon ase neki?)
A. Service to the society and the nation.	উত্তৰ ঃ	মই সমাজ আৰু ৰাষ্ট্ৰৰ সেৱা কৰিব বিচাৰো । (Moi xomaj aru rastror xewar koribo bisaro.)
Q. Quite happy to know your ideas. May God help you!	প্ৰশ্ন ঃ	তোমাৰ কথাবোৰ শুনি বৰ ভাল লাগিল । ভগবানে তোমাৰ সহায় কৰক । (Tomar kothabor xuni bor bhal lagil. Bhogobane tomar xohai korok.)

4. TALKING TO A BOY

এজন ল'ৰাৰ সৈতে কথা-বতৰা

(aejon loror xoite kotha-botora)

Man :	Will you help me?	ব্যক্তি ঃ মোক অলপ সহায় কৰিবানে ? (Mok olop xohai koribane?)
Boy :	Why not!	ল'ৰা ঃ কিয় নকৰিম ! (Kiyo nokorim!)
Man :	Thanks.	ব্যক্তি ঃ ধন্যবাদ (Dhonyobad)
Boy :	Anything else?	ল'ৰা ঃ আৰু কিবা ? (Aru kiba?)
Man :	No, please.	ব্যক্তি ঃ নাই, হ'ব । (Nai, hobo.)
Boy :	O.K.	ল'ৰা ঃ ঠিক আছে । (Thik ase.)
Man :	What is your name?	ব্যক্তি ঃ তোমাৰ নাম কি ? (Tomar naam ki?)
Boy :	Pranjit Kakoti	ল'ৰা ঃ প্ৰাণজিত কাকতি ।
Man :	What do you do?	ব্যক্তি ঃ তুমি কি কৰা ? (Tumi ki kora?)
Boy :	I am studying, sir.	ল'ৰা ঃ মই পঢ়ি আছোঁ, মহাশয় । (Moi porhi aso, mohaxoi)
Man :	In which school?	ব্যক্তি ঃ কোন স্কুলত ? (Kon skulot?)
Boy :	Not in school, but in college.	ল'ৰা ঃ স্কুলত নহয়, কলেজত । (Sukulot nohoi, kolejot)

Man :	Very good! In which year are you?	ব্যক্তি ঃ	বাঃ ! তুমি এতিয়া কোন বৰ্ষত ? (Bah! Tumi etiya kon borxot?)
Boy :	B.A., first year.	ল'ৰা ঃ	বি.এ., প্ৰথম বৰ্ষত। (Bi e., prothom borxot)
Man :	In which college are you studying?	ব্যক্তি ঃ	তুমি কোন কলেজত পঢ়া ? (Tumi kon kolejot porha?)
Boy :	In Cotton College.	ল'ৰা ঃ	কটন কলেজত। (Cotton kolejot)
Man :	That is a very famous college.	ব্যক্তি ঃ	সেইখন এখন বিখ্যাত কলেজ। (Xeikhon aekhon bikhyat kolej.)
Boy :	Yes, sir.	ল'ৰা ঃ	হয়, মহাশয়। (Hoi, mohaxoi)
Man :	How far is the college from your home?	ব্যক্তি ঃ	তোমাৰ ঘৰৰ পৰা কলেজলৈ কিমান দূৰ ? (Tomar ghoror pora kolejoloi kiman door?)
Boy :	Nearly ten kilometres.	ল'ৰা ঃ	প্ৰায় দহ কিলোমিটাৰ। (Prai doh kilomitar)
Man :	It must be taking you a long time to reach your college?	ব্যক্তি ঃ	কলেজ গৈ পাওঁতে তোমাৰ নিশ্চয় বহুত সময় লাগে ? (Kolej goi pawnte tomar nissoi bohut xomoi lage?)
Boy :	Yes, Sir; at least one hour.	ল'ৰা ঃ	হয় মহাশয়; কমেও এঘন্টা লাগে। (Hoi, mohaxoi; komeo

			aeghonta lage.)
Man :	When does your College start?	ব্যক্তি ঃ	তোমাৰ কলেজ কিমান সময়ত আৰম্ভ হয় ? (Tomar kolej kiman xomoyot arombho hoi?)
Boy :	At nine in the morning.	ল'ৰা ঃ	পুৱা ন বজাত। (Puwa no bojat)
Man :	How many students are there in your college?	ব্যক্তি ঃ	তোমালোকৰ কলেজত কিমান ছাত্ৰ-ছাত্ৰী আছে ? (Tomalokor kolejot kiman satro-satri ase?)
Boy :	Nearly two thousand.	ল'ৰা ঃ	প্ৰায় দুহেজাৰ। (Prai duhezar)
Man :	And professors?	ব্যক্তি ঃ	আৰু অধ্যাপক ? (Aru odhyapok?)
Boy :	More than one hundred	ল'ৰা ঃ	এশ জনতকৈও বেছি। (Aexo jonot koio besi)
Man :	Do you play any game?	ব্যক্তি ঃ	তুমি কিবা খেল খেলা নেকি ? (Tumi kiba khael khaela neki?)
Boy :	Yes, football.	ল'ৰা ঃ	হয়, ফুটবল খেলোঁ। (Hoi, futbol khaelo.)
Man :	O.K., friend. Wish you best of luck.	ব্যক্তি ঃ	বাৰু, বন্ধু, বিদায়। তোমাৰ ভবিষ্যত উজ্জ্বল হওক। (Baaru, bondhu, bidai. Tomar bhobishyot ujjwol howk.)

5. CONVERSATION BETWEEN TWO FRIENDS

দুজন বন্ধুৰ মাজত কথা-বতৰা

(dujon bondhur majot kotha-botora)

Tarun :	Hallo Ranjit, how do you do?	তৰুণ ঃ	আৰে ৰঞ্জিত, কি খবৰ ? (Are ronjit, ki khobor?)
Ranjit :	Fine, what about you?	ৰঞ্জিত ঃ	ভালে আছো। তোৰ খবৰ ক চোন। (Bhale aso. Tor khobor ko son)
Tarun :	I am also alright.	তৰুণ ঃ	ময়ো ভালেই আছো। (Moyo bhalei aso.)
Ranjit :	Is everyone well at home?	ৰঞ্জিত ঃ	ঘৰত সকলোৰে ভালনে ? (Ghorot xokolore bhalne?)
Tarun :	Yes, all is well.	তৰুণ ঃ	অঁ, সকলোৰে ভাল। (On, xokolore bhal)
Ranjit :	Where are you going?	ৰঞ্জিত ঃ	তই ক'লৈ যাব ? (Toi koloi jawo?)
Tarun :	I am going to my college.	তৰুণ ঃ	মই কলেজলৈ যাওঁ। (Moi kolejoloi jawn)
Ranjit :	But today is a holiday.	ৰঞ্জিত ঃ	কিন্তু আজি তো বন্ধ। (Kintu ajit to bondho.)
Tarun :	The library is open.	তৰুণ ঃ	লাইব্ৰেৰী খোলা আছে। (Laibreri khola ase.)
Ranjit :	Will you study there?	ৰঞ্জিত ঃ	তই তাত পঢ়িবি নেকি ?

			(Toi tat porhibi neki?)
Tarun :	No, I will not study there.	তৰুণ ঃ	নাই, মই তাত নপঢ়ো। (Nai, moi tat noporho.)
Ranjit :	Then?	ৰঞ্জিত ঃ	তেন্তে ? (Tente?)
Tarun :	I want to borrow some books.	তৰুণ ঃ	মই কেইখনমান কিতাপ আনোগৈ। (Moi keikhonman kitap anogoi)
Ranjit :	Let's talk for a few minutes.	ৰঞ্জিত ঃ	আহ অলপ সময় কথাকে পাতো। (Ah, olop xomoi kothake pato)
Tarun :	We have met after a very long time.	তৰুণ ঃ	বহুত দিনৰ মূৰত লগ পালো, ভাই। (Bohut dinor murot log palo bhai)
Ranjit :	In which college are you studying?	ৰঞ্জিত ঃ	তই কোন কলেজত পঢ় ? (Toi kon kolejot porho?)
Tarun :	Pragyotish College, you?	তৰুণ ঃ	প্ৰাগজ্যোতিষ কলেজত, তই ? (Pragjyotish kolejot, toi?)
Ranjit :	B. Barua College. I am a student of B.A., 2nd year.	ৰঞ্জিত ঃ	বি বৰুৱা কলেজত। মই বি.এ., দ্বিতীয় বৰ্ষত আছো। (bi borua kolejot. Moi Bi. e. dwitiyo borxot aso.)

Tarun :	I am also in B.A., 2nd year.	তৰুণ ঃ	ময়ো বি.এ., দ্বিতীয় বৰ্ষত আছো। (Moyo bi.e. dwitiyo borxot aso
Ranjit :	Where are you living nowadays?	ৰঞ্জিত ঃ	তই আজিকালি ক'ত থাক ? (Toi ajikali kot thako?)
Tarun :	In Jalukbari, near the university.	তৰুণ ঃ	জালুকবাৰীত, বিশ্ববিদ্যালয়ৰ ওচৰত। (Jalukbarit, bishwobidyaloyor osorot)
Ranjit :	Are you staying in the same place?	ৰঞ্জিত ঃ	তই আগৰ ঠাইতেই আছে নে ? (Toi agor thaitei asone?)
Tarun :	Yes, there only.	তৰুণ ঃ	অঁ, তাতেই আছো। (On, tatei aso)
Ranjit :	If you have some spare time, lets go to the coffee house and have a cup of coffee.	ৰঞ্জিত ঃ	তোৰ হাতত যদি সময় আছে, তেন্তে কফি হাউচলৈ গৈ একাপ একাপ কফি খাওঁগৈ ব'ল। (Tor hatot jodi xomoi ase, tente kofi hausoloi goi aekap aekap kofi khaongoi boi)

6. GETTING READY FOR OFFICE

অফিচলৈ যোৱাৰ প্ৰস্তুতি

(ofisoloi jowar prostuti)

Wife :	Please get up, darling, you are getting late for your office.	পত্নী ঃ উঠা, প্ৰিয়তম। তোমাৰ অফিচলৈ যোৱা দেৰি হ'ব। (Utha priyotom. Tomar offisoloi jowa deri hobo.)
Husband :	Please don't disturb me. Let me sleep for sometime more.	পতি ঃ আমনি নকৰিবাচোন। মোক আৰু অলপ শুবলৈ দিয়া। (Amoni nokoribason. Mok aru olop xuboloi diya.)
Wife :	Are you not goint to your office today?	পত্নী ঃ তুমি আজি অফিচলৈ নোযোৱা নেকি ? (Tumi aji ofisoloi nojowa neki?)
Husband :	Why should I not? What's the time?	পতি ঃ কিয় নাযাম ? সময় কিমান হ'ল ? (Kiyo najam? Xomoi Kiman hol?)
Wife :	Get up, then; it's seven	পত্নী ঃ উঠা তেন্তে; সাত বাজিল। (Utha tente; xat bajil)

Husband :	Oh! It's seven!	পতি ঃ অ'ঃ ! সাত বাজিলে ! (Oh! xat bajile!).
Wife :	Make haste, otherwise you won't get your bus.	পত্নী ঃ লৰালৰি কৰা । নহ'লে তোমাৰ বাছ নাপাবাগৈ । (Loralori kora. Nohole tomar bas napabagoi)
Husband :	I must get up at once, because I have to reach my office exactly at 9 a.m.	পতি ঃ মই এইমাত্ৰই উঠিব লাগিব, কাৰণ মই ঠিক ন বজাতে অফিচ গৈ পাবই লাগিব । (Moi eimatroi uthibo lagibo, karon moi thik no bojate ofis goi paboi lagibo.)
Wife :	All right, please get up now.	পত্নী ঃ ঠিক আছে, উঠা এতিয়া । (Thik ase, utha etiya.)
Husband :	Who is in the bathroom?	পতি ঃ বাথৰুমত কোন আছে ? (bathroomot kon ase?)
Wife :	Nobody. You go to the bathroom, I am preparing your breakfast.	পত্নী ঃ কোনো নাই । তুমি বাথৰুমলৈ যোৱা, মই তোমাৰ জলপান তৈয়াৰ তৈয়াৰ কৰো । (Kono nai. Tumi bathroomoloi jowa, moi tomar jolpan toyar koro)

Husband :	A cup of tea before that.	পতি ঃ তাৰ আগতে একাপ চাহ । (tar agote aekap sah)
Wife :	Here's your tea. I've already prepared it.	পত্নী ঃ এয়া লোৱা চাহ । মই বনায়েই থৈছো । (Eya lowa sah. moi bonayei thoiso.)
Husband :	Oh, good!	পতি ঃ বঢ়িয়া ! (borhiya!)
Wife :	Listen, if you want tea first, then you must get up at 6 a.m.	পত্নী ঃ শুনা, যদি তোমাক আগতে চাহ লাগে, তেনে হ'লে তুমি ছয় বজাত উঠিব লাগিব । (Xuna, jodi tomak agote sah lage, tenehole tumisoi bojat uthibo lagibo.)
Husband :	O.K., I, shall take care, but where is my brush and tooth paste?	পতি ঃ ঠিক আছে, মনত ৰাখিম বাৰু । কিন্তু মোৰ ব্ৰাছ ডাল আৰু টুথপেষ্টটো ক'ত ? (Thik ase, monot rakhim baru. kintu mor brash dal aru toothpesto kot?
Wife :	Go to the bathroom. Everything is lying near the wash basin.	পত্নী ঃ বাথৰুমলৈ যোৱা । চব বেচিনৰ ওচৰতে আছে । (Bathroomoloi jowa.

		sob besinor osorote ase.)
Husband :	O.K., madam, I am Coming in five minutes.	পতি ঃ ঠিক আছে মেডাম, মই পাঁচ মিনিটতে আহিম। (Thik ase maedam, moi pans minitote ahim.)
Wife :	Come fast, breakfast is ready.	পত্নী ঃ খৰধৰ কৰা, জলপান সাজু কৰি থৈছো। (Khordhor kora, tomar jolpan xazu kori thoiso.)
Husband :	Here I am, where is my breakfast?	পতি ঃ মই অহিলো, ক'তা মোৰ জলপান ? (Moi, ahilo, kota mor jolpan?
Wife :	Just bringing, dear!	পত্নী ঃ এতিয়াই আনিছোঁ, প্ৰিয়তম ! (Etiyai aniso, priyotom!)
Husband :	Thanks!	পতি ঃ ধন্যবাদ ! (dhonyobad!)
Wife :	I hope it has not become cold.	পত্নী ঃ ঠাণ্ডা হৈ যোৱা নাই চাগে'। (Thanda hoi jowa nai sage.)
Husband :	No, no, it's quite hot	পতি ঃ নাই, নাই, বেছ গৰম

		হৈ আছে। (Nai nai, bes gorom hoi ase.)
Wife :	You have your breakfast, I am preparing your lunch box.	পত্নী ঃ তুমি খোৱা, মই তোমাৰ দুপৰীয়াৰ আহাৰৰ টোপোলাটো বান্ধোঁ। (Tumi khowa, moi tomar duporiyar aharor topolato bandho)
Husband :	You better hurry up. I have to reach office early today.	পতি ঃ খৰধৰ কৰা। আজি মই অলপ সোনকালে অফিচ পাবগৈ লাগে। (Khordhor kora. aji moi alop xonkale ofis pabogoi lage.)
Wife :	Here are your shoes and shirt.	পত্নী ঃ এয়া তোমাৰ জোতা আৰু চোলা। (Eya tomar zota aru sola)
Husband :	Thanks.	পতি ঃ ধন্যবাদ। (Dhonyobad)
Wife :	And here is your file.	পত্নী ঃ আৰু এইটো তোমাৰ ফাইল। (Aru eito tomar fail)
Husband :	Why hasn't Chintu Left for school yet?	পতি ঃ চিন্তু এতিয়াও স্কুললৈ যোৱা নাই কিয় ?

		(Chintu etiyao skuloloi jowa nai kiyo?)
Wife :	He is just having milk.	পত্নী ঃ সি গাখীৰ খাই আছে। (Xi gakhir khai ase)
Husband :	Have you kept my lunch box?	পতি ঃ মোৰ লাঞ্চ বক্সটো দিছানে ? (Mor lanch boks to disane?
Wife :	Yes!	পত্নী ঃ অঁ! (On!)
Husband :	O.K., now I must leave.	পতি ঃ ঠিক আছে, মই যাওঁ। (Thik ase, moi jawn.)
Wife :	Come back in time in the evening.	পত্নী ঃ গধূলি সময়মতে ঘূৰি আহিবা। (Godhuli xomoimote ghuri ahiba.)
Husband :	O.K., bye-bye.	পতি ঃ বাৰু, বাই-বাই। (Baaru, bai-bai.)
Wife :	Bye-bye!	পত্নী ঃ বাই-বাই ! (Bai-bai)

7. ARRIVAL OF A GUEST

এজন আলহীৰ আগমন

(aejon alohir agomon)

Raktim :	Whom do you want to meet, sir?	ৰক্তিম ঃ	আপুনি কাক লগ পাব বিচাৰিছে, মহাশয় ? (apuni kaak log pabo bisarise, mohaxoi?)
Guest :	I have to meet Mr. Barua. I've come from Delhi.	আলহী ঃ	মই শ্ৰীবৰুৱাক লগ পাব বিচাৰিছো। মই দিল্লীৰ আহিছো। (oi sri boruak log pabo bisariso, moi dillir pora ahiso.)
Raktim :	Your good name, Sir?	ৰক্তিম ঃ	আপোনাৰ নামটো জানিব পাৰোঁনে, মহাশয় ? (aponar namto janibo parone, mohaxoi?
Guest :	My name is Sachin Verma.	আলহী ঃ	মোৰ নাম শচীন ৱাৰ্মা। (mor nam sachin verma)
Raktim :	Please come in and be seated. I'll just call my father.	ৰক্তিম ঃ	অনুগ্ৰহ কৰি ভিতৰলৈ আহক আৰু বহক। মই এতিয়াই দেউতাক মাতি দিছো। (onugroh kori

			bhitoroloi ahok aru bohok. moi etiyai deutak mati diso)
Guest :	Thank you.	আলহী ঃ	ধন্যবাদ।
			(dhonyobad.)
Mr. Barua :	Hallo, Mr. Verma! How are you?	বৰুৱা ঃ	হেল্ল' মিস্টাৰ বাৰ্মা ! কি খবৰ ? ভালনে ?
			(haello mistar varma! ki khobor?bhalne?)
Mr. Verma :	Hallo, Mr. Barua! I amfine, what about you?	বাৰ্মা ঃ	হেল্ল' মিস্টাৰ বৰুৱা ! মোৰ ভালেই। আপুনি কেনে আছে ?
			(haello mistar borua! mor bhalei. apuni kaenae ase?)
Barua :	I am also fine. Was your journey Comfortable or not?	বৰুৱা ঃ	মোৰো ভাল। আপোনাৰ যাত্ৰা আৰামদায়ক আছিল নে ?
			(moro bhal. aponar jatra aramdayok asil ne?)
Guest :	Not quite. The train was three hours late.	আলহী ঃ	ঠিক আৰামদায়ক বুলিব নোবাৰি। গাড়ী তিনিঘণ্টা পলমকৈ পাইছেহি।
			(thik aramdayok bulibo nowari. gari tinighonta polomkoi

			paisehi.)
Barua :	But the train started in time from Delhi?	বৰুৱা ঃ	কিন্তু ট্ৰেইন দিল্লীৰ পৰা ঠিক সময়তে এৰিছিল ? (kintu trein dillir pora thik xomoyote erisil?)
Guest :	Yes, but there was a mishap on the way. That is why it was delayed.	আলহী ঃ	হয়, কিন্তু মাজবাটতে এটা দুৰ্ঘটনা হোৱাৰ কাৰণে গাড়ী পলম হৈ গ'ল। (hoi, kintu mazbatote aeta durghotona howar karone gari polom hoi gol.)
Barua :	Was it serious?	বৰুৱা ঃ	ডাঙৰ কিবা দুৰ্ঘটনা হৈছিল নেকি ? (dangor kiba durghotona hoisil neki?
Guest :	Not at all; please don't worry.	আলহী ঃ	নাই, ডাঙৰ একো হোৱা নাছিল, চিন্তা নকৰিব। (nai, dangor aeko howa nasil, sinta nokoribo.)
Barua :	Now, you wash yourself. You must be quite tired.	বৰুৱা ঃ	আপুনি হাত-মুখ ধুই লওক। আপোনাৰ নিশ্চয় বেছ ভাগৰ লাগিছে।

			(apuni hat-mukh dhui lowk. aponar nissoi bes bhagor lagise.)
Guest :	Yes, please show me the bathroom.	আলহী ঃ	হয়, মোক বাথৰুমটো দেখুৱাই দিয়কচোন। (hoi, mok bathroom to dekhuwai diyokson.)
Barua :	Raktim will show you. The soap and towel are already kept there.	বৰুৱা ঃ	ৰক্তিমে আপোনাক দেখুৱাই দিব। চাবোন আৰু গামোছা তাতে আছে। (roktime aponak dekhuwai dibo. sabon aru gamosa tate ase.)
Guest :	Thanks.	আলহী ঃ	ধন্যবাদ। (dhonyobad)
Barua :	You make yourself fresh. In the meantime I shall ask my wife to lay the table for lunch.	বৰুৱা ঃ	আপুনি সতেজ হৈ লওক। ইতিমধ্যে মই মোৰ পৰিবাৰক ভাত খোৱাৰ আয়োজন কৰিবলৈ কওঁ। (apuni xotez hoi lowk. itimodhye moi mor 'poribarok bhat khowar ayojon koriboloi kown)
Guest :	O.K., I'm just coming.	আলহী ঃ	ভাল বাৰু। মই এতিয়াই আহিছো। (bhal baru. moi etiyai ahiso)

BOOKING A TRUNK CALL

ট্ৰাঙ্ককল বুক কৰা

(trank kol buk kora)

Subscriber :	Hallo, exchange?	গ্ৰাহক ঃ	হেল্ল', এক্সচেঞ্জ ? (haello, ekschenj?)
Operator :	Yes, speaking.	অপাৰেটৰ ঃ	হয়, কৈছো। (hoi, koiso)
Subscriber :	Madam, I want to book a trunk call	গ্ৰাহক ঃ	মেডাম, মই এটা ট্ৰাঙ্ককল বুক কৰিব খুজিছো। (maedam, moi aeta trankkol buk koribo khujiso.)
Operator :	What is your telephone number sir?	অপাৰেটৰ ঃ	আপোনাৰ ফোন নম্বৰটো কওকচোন। (aponar phon numborto kowkson.)
Subscriber :	My telephone number is 55-1854	গ্ৰাহক ঃ	মোৰ ফোন নম্বৰ ৫৫-১৮৫৪ (mor phon nombor 55-1854)
Operator :	for which city, sir?	অপাৰেটৰ ঃ	কোন চহৰ লাগে আপোনাক ? (kon shor lage aponak?)

Subscriber :	For Delhi, please.	গ্ৰাহক ঃ	দিল্লী (dilli)
Operator :	Please give me, the Delhi number.	অপাৰেটৰ ঃ	দিল্লীৰ নম্বৰটো দিয়কচোন। (dillir nombor to diyokson)
Subscriber :	5430506	গ্ৰাহক ঃ	৫৪৩০৫০৬ (5430506)
Operator :	Is it a P.P. call? Whom do you want to speak to?	অপাৰেটৰ ঃ	এইটো কোনোবা বিশেষ ব্যক্তিৰ নামৰ কল নেকি ? আপুনি কাৰ লগত কথা পাতিব খুজিছে ? (eito konoba bixex byoktir namor kol neki? apuni kar logot kotha patibo khujise?)
Subscriber :	I want to speak to Mr. Ramen Kalita	গ্ৰাহক ঃ	মই শ্ৰীৰমেন কলিতাৰ লগত কথা পাতিব খুজিছো। (moi sri romen kolitar logot kotha patibo khujiso.)
Operator :	Your Registration No. is B-682	অপাৰেটৰ ঃ	আপোনাৰ ৰেজিষ্ট্ৰেশ্যন নম্বৰ হ'ল বি-৬৮২ (aponar registreshon nombor hol bi-682)
Subscriber :	Please tell me	গ্ৰাহক ঃ	অনুগ্ৰহ কৰি আকৌ এবাৰ

	once again.		কওকচোন। (onugroh kori akou aebar kowkson)
Operator :	B-682; B for Bombay.	অপাৰেটৰ ঃ	বি-৬৮২; বি ফৰ বম্বে। (bi-682; bi for bombay)
Subscriber :	Thank you. When can I get it?	গ্ৰাহক ঃ	ধন্যবাদ। কেতিয়া লাইন পাম ?
Operator :	It may take one hour.	অপাৰেটৰ ঃ	এঘন্টা লাগিব পাৰে। (aeghonta lagibo pare)
Subscriber :	O.K., I am waiting.	গ্ৰাহক ঃ	হ'ব বাৰু, মই অপেক্ষা কৰিছো। (hobo baru, moi opekhya koriso)

(After one Hour)

এঘন্টাৰ পাছত

(aeghontar pasot)

Operator :	Hallo, is it 55-1854?	অপাৰেটৰ ঃ	হেল্ল', ৫৫১৮৫৪ নেকি ? (haello, 551854 neki?)
Subscriber :	Yes, speaking	গ্ৰাহক ঃ	হয়, কৈছোঁ।. (hoi, koiso)
Operator :	Here is your P.P. call to Delhi. Please talk.	অপাৰেটৰ ঃ	এয়া আপোনাৰ দিল্লীৰ কল। কথা পাতক। (eya aponar dillir kol. kotha patok.)
Subscriber :	Thanks, madam.	গ্ৰাহক ঃ	ধন্যবাদ, মেডাম। (dhonyobad, maedom)

	After three minutes		তিনি মিনিটৰ পাছত (tini minitor pasot)
Operator :	Three minutes are over.	অপাৰেটৰ ঃ	তিনি মিনিট হৈ গৈছে। (tini minit hoi goise)
Subscriber :	Please extend time. Don't disconnect.	গ্ৰাহক ঃ	অনুগ্ৰহ কৰি সময় বঢ়াই দিয়ক, নাকাটিব। (onugroh kori xomoi borhai diyok, nakatibo.)
Operator :	O.K.	অপাৰেটৰ ঃ	ঠিক আছে। (thik ase)
	After concluding the talk		**কথা শেষ হোৱাৰ পাছত (kotha xex howar pasot)**
Subscriber :	Hallo, madam. The talk is over. Could you kindly let me know the charge?	গ্ৰাহক ঃ	হেল্ল' মেডাম, কথা পতা হৈ গ'ল; অনুগ্ৰহ কৰি চাৰ্জ কিমান হ'ল কওক চোন। (haello, madam, kotha pota hoi gol. onugroh kori charj kiman hol kowkson)

9. AT THE GENERAL STORE

বিবিধ সামগ্ৰীৰ দোকানত

(bibidh xamogrir dokanot)

Salesman :	What can I do for you sir?	দোকানী ঃ	আপোনাক কেনেকৈ সহায় কৰিব পাৰোঁ, মহাশয় ? (aponak kaenaekoi xohai koribo paron mohaxoi?)
Customer :	Do you have 'Key' detergent powder?	গ্ৰাহক ঃ	আপোনাৰ দোকানত 'কী' ডিটাৰজেন্ট পাউডাৰ আছে নে ? (aponar dokanot kee ditarjent paudar ase ne?)
Salesman :	Yes, sir, here it is.	দোকানী ঃ	হয়, আছে; এয়া লওক। (hoi, ase; eya lowk)
Customer :	Please give me one more packet.	গ্ৰাহক ঃ	আৰু এপেকেট দিয়ক চোন। (aru aepaekaet diyok son)
Salesman :	As you wish.	দোকানী ঃ	আপুনি যি কয়। (apuni ji koi)
Customer :	How much do I have to pay?	গ্ৰাহক ঃ	মই কিমান দিব লাগিব ? (moi kiman dibo lagibo?)
Salesman :	Just twenty-six	দোকানী ঃ	মাত্ৰ ছাব্বিশ টকা, মহাশয়।

	rupees, sir.		(matro sabbis toka, mohaxoi)
Customer :	Here is your money.	গ্ৰাহক ঃ	এয়া লওক পইচা। (eya lowk poisa.)
Salesman :	Thanks! Anything else?	দোকানী ঃ	ধন্যবাদ ! আৰু কিবা লাগিব ? (dhonyobad! aru kiba lagibo?)
Customer :	No, no, that was all I wanted.	গ্ৰাহক ঃ	নাই, নালাগে; কেৱল এইটোৰেই দৰকাৰ আছিল। (nai, nalage; kewol eitorei dorkar asil.)
Salesman :	Thanks! Visit again.	দোকানী ঃ	ধন্যবাদ ! আকৌ আহিব। (dhonyobad! akou ahibo.)

10. OPENING A BANK ACCOUNT
বেঙ্কত একাউণ্ট খোলা
(baenkot aekaunt khola)

Customer :	I want to see the manager.	গ্ৰাহক ঃ	মই মেনেজাৰক লগ পাব বিচাৰিছো। (moi maenaejarok log pabo bisariso.)

Bank employee :	Please come here. Meet Mr. Manager	বেঙ্কৰ কৰ্মচাৰী ঃ	এইফালে আহক। এখেতেই হ'ল মেনেজাৰ। (eiphale ahok. ekhetei hol maenaejar)
Manager :	(Shaking hands) What can I do for you?	মেনেজাৰঃ	(কৰমৰ্দন কৰি) মই আপোনাৰ বাবে কি কৰিব পাৰোঁ ? moi aponar babe ki koribo paron?
Customer :	I want to open a savings account.	গ্ৰাহক ঃ	মই এটা চেভিংচ একাউণ্ট খুলিব খুজিছোঁ। (moi aeta sevings ackaunt khulibo khujiso)
Manager :	With great pleasure, (to employee) please bring savings-account papers.	মেনেজাৰঃ	বৰ ভাল কথা, (কৰ্মচাৰীক) চেভিংচ একাউণ্টৰ কাগজ-পত্ৰ আনকচোন। (bor bhal kotha, sevings aekaunto kagoz potro anokson)
Customer :	Thanks, what amount is needed to open a savings accounts?	গ্ৰাহক ঃ	ধন্যবাদ। চেভিংচ একাউণ্ট খুলিবলৈ কিমান টকা লাগে ? (dhonyobad, sevings aekaunt khuliboloi kiman toka lage?)

Manager :	You can open a savings account with an initial deposit of fifty rupees.	মেনেজাৰঃ	আপুনি প্ৰথমে পঞ্চাশ টকা জমা কৰি চেভিংচ একাউন্ট খুলিব পাৰে। (apuni prothome ponchas toka joma kori sevings aekaunt khulibo pare.)
Customer :	I want to open a joint account with my wife.	গ্ৰাহক ঃ	মই মোৰ পত্নীৰ সৈতে এটা জইন্ট একাউন্ট খুলিব খুজিছো। (moi mor potnir xoite aeta joint aekaunt khulibo khujiso)
Manager :	Is your wife also here with you?	মেনেজাৰঃ	আপোনাৰ পত্নীও আপোনাৰ লগতে আহিছে নেকি ? (aponar potnio aponar logote ahise neki?)
Customer :	No, she is not here at the moment. But I can bring her here after sometime	গ্ৰাহক ঃ	তেওঁ ইয়ালৈ অহা নাই। নাই। কিন্তু মই তেওঁক অলপ পাছত লৈ আহিব পাৰিম। (teon iyaloi oha nai, kintu moi teonk olop pasot loi ahibo parim)
Manager :	O.K. Her presence is essential, but I	মেনেজাৰঃ	হ'ব বাৰু। তেখেত উপস্হিত থকাটো জৰুৰী;

	can give you the forms for opening an account.		অৱশ্যে মই আপোনাক একাউন্ট খোলাৰ প্ৰ-পত্ৰ দিব পাৰোঁ। (hobo baru. tekhet uposthit thokato zoruri; obosye moi aponak aekaunt kholar pro-potro dib paron)
Customer :	I would like to have a cheque-book also.	গ্ৰাহক ঃ	মই চেক-বুকো ল'ব খুজিছোঁ। (moi chek-buko lobo khujiso)
Manager :	You can have a cheque-book; but there must be a minimum balance of Rs. 100/- all the time.	মেনেজাৰঃ	আপুনি চেক বুক ল'ব পাৰে, কিন্তু তাৰ কাৰণে আপোনাৰ একাউন্টত সকলো সময়তে কমেও ১০০ টকা থাকিব লাগিব। (apuni chek buk lobo pare, kintu tar karone aponar aekauntot xokolo xomoyote komeo aexo toka thakibo lagibo)

Customer :	That's right. I've understood.	গ্ৰাহক ঃ	হয়, মই বুজি পাইছো। (hoi, moi buji paiso)
Manager :	Take the forms, bring them duly filled in alongwith your photographs. Your account will be opened.	মেনেজাৰঃ	এই কাগজ পত্ৰখিনি লওক। এইখিনি পূৰাই আপোনালোকৰ ফটোৰ সৈতে লৈ আনিব; আপোনাৰ একাউন্ট খোলা হৈ যাব। (ei kagoz potrokhini lowk. eikhini purai aponalokor photore xoite loi anibo; aponar aekaunt khola hoi jabo.)
Customer :	Thanks.	গ্ৰাহক ঃ	ধন্যবাদ। (dhonyobad)

11. ASKING THE ADDRESS

(thikona bisora)

Robin :	Do you live here?	ৰবীন ঃ	আপুনি ইয়াতে থাকে নেকি ? (apuni iyate thake neki?)

Victor : Yes, tell me what can I do for you.	ভিক্টৰ ঃ হয়, কওকচোন মই আপোনাৰ বাবে কি কৰিব পাৰোঁ। (hoi, kowkson moi aponar babe ki korib paron.)
Robin : I am a stranger in Guwahati. Could you tell me where is Paltan Bazar?	ৰবীন ঃ মই গুৱাহাটীত নতুন। পল্টন বজাৰ কোনফালে মোক দেখুৱাই দিবনে ? (moi guwahatit notum. polton bozar konphale mokdekhuwaidibone?)
Victor : Yes, certainly, It is just behind the railway station. You have to cross the over bridge.	ভিক্টৰ ঃ হয়, নিশ্চয়। ৰেল ষ্টেচন-টোৰ ঠিক পিছফালেই আছে পল্টন বজাৰ। আপুনি মাত্ৰ অ'ভাৰব্ৰীজখন পাৰ হ'ব লাগিব। (hoi, nissoi. rel stesontor thik pisphalei ase polton bozar apuni matro overbrij khon par hobo lagibo.)
Robin : This is the address I want to go to.	ৰবীন ঃ মই এই ঠিকনাটোলৈ যাব খুজিছোঁ। (moi ei thikonatoloi jabo khujison)
Victor : Well, you will have	ভিক্টৰ ঃ অ', আপুনি উলুবাৰীলৈ

	to go to Ulubari; that is, beyond Paltan Bazar.		যাব লাগিব; মানে, পল্টন বজাৰৰ পৰা আৰু আগলৈ। (O, apuni ulubariloi jabo lagibo; mane, polton bozaror pora aru agoloi)
Robin :	Yes, yes.		

12. FACING AN INTERVIEW
ইন্টাৰভিউ দিবলৈ যোৱা
(intarviu diboloi jowa)

Candidate :	(Hurriedly) Has the interview started?	প্ৰাৰ্থী ঃ	(খৰধৰকৈ) ইন্টাৰভিউ আৰম্ভ হৈ গ'ল নেকি ? intarviu arombho hoi gol neki?
Peon :	Yes, sir, about half-an-hour ago.	পিয়ন ঃ	হয়, মহাশয়। আধা ঘন্টাৰ আগতেই। (hoi, mohaxoi.adha ghontar agotei)
Candidate :	My name is Baben Dutta. Have I not been called yet?	প্ৰাৰ্থী ঃ	মোৰ নাম ভবেন দত্ত। মোৰ নাম এতিয়ালৈকে মতা নাই তো ? (mor nam bhaben dotto. mor nam

			etiyaloike mota naito?)
Peon :	Not yet, but after this it is your turn.	পিয়ন ঃ	এতিয়ালৈকে মতা নাই, কিন্তু ইয়াৰ পাছতে আপোনাৰ পাল। (etlyaloike mota nai, kintu iyar pasote aponar pal.)
Candidate :	Oh! I am in time.	প্ৰাৰ্থী ঃ	উঃ ! মই ঠিক সময়তে পাইছোহি। (uh! moi thik xomoyote paisohi)
Peon :	Not in time, you are late. Be careful in future.	পিয়ন ঃ	ঠিক সময়ত নহয়, আপুনি দেৰিকৈ পাইছেহি। আগলৈ সাবধান হ'ব। (thik xomoyot nohi, apuni derikoi paisehi. agoloi xabodhan hobo)
Candidate :	O.K., brother I shall be.	প্ৰাৰ্থী ঃ	ঠিকেই কৈছা, ভাই। সাবধান হ'ম। (thikei koisa bhai. xabodhan hom.)
Candidate :	May I come in, sir?	প্ৰাৰ্থী ঃ	সোমাব পাৰোঁনে, মহাশয় ? (xomabo parone, mohaxoi?)
Officer :	Yes, please come in.	বিষয়া ঃ	হয়, আহক। (hoi, ahok.)
Candidate :	Good morning, sir.	প্ৰাৰ্থী ঃ	সুপ্ৰভাত, মহাশয়।

			(xuprobhat, mohaxoi)
Officer :	Good morning, please be seated.	বিষয়া ঃ	সুপ্ৰভাত, বহক । (xuprobhat, bohok)
Candidate :	Thank you!	প্ৰাৰ্থী ঃ	ধন্যবাদ ! (dhonyobad!)
Officer :	What is your name?	বিষয়া ঃ	আপোনাৰ নাম ? (aponar nam?)
Candidate :	My name is Bhaben Dutta.	প্ৰাৰ্থী ঃ	মোৰ নাম ভবেন দত্ত । (mor nam bhoben dotto)
Officer :	What is your educational qualification?	বিষয়া ঃ	আপোনাৰ শিক্ষাগত অৰ্হতা কি ? (aponar xikhyagoto orhota ki?)
Candidate :	I passed my M.A. this year.	প্ৰাৰ্থী ঃ	মই এইবছৰ এম.এ. পাছ কৰিছোঁ । (moi eibosor em.e. pass koriso)
Officer :	From which University?	বিষয়া ঃ	কোন বিশ্ববিদ্যালয়ৰ পৰা ? (kon bishwobidyaloyor pora?)
Candidate :	From Dibrugarh University.	প্ৰাৰ্থী ঃ	ডিব্ৰুগড় বিশ্ববিদ্যালয়ৰ পৰা । (dibrugor bishwobidyaloyor pora.)
Officer :	What is your hobby?	বিষয়া ঃ	আপোনাৰ হবি কি ? (aponar hobi ki?)

Candiate :	Painting, sir.	প্ৰাৰ্থী ঃ	চিত্ৰকলা, মহাশয়। (sitrokola, mohaxoi)
Officer :	But I think painting is a costly hobby.	বিষয়া ঃ	কিন্তু চিত্ৰকলাৰ হবিটো খৰচী, নহয়নে ? (kintu sitrokolar hobi to khorosi, nohoine?)
Candidate :	Yes, sir, it is very costly.	প্ৰাৰ্থী ঃ	হয় মহাশয়, ই বৰ খৰচী। (hoi mohaxoi, i bor khorosi)
Officer :	Why do you want a job in a college?	বিষয়া ঃ	আপুনি কলেজৰ চাকৰি কিয় কৰিব বিচাৰিছে ? (apuni kolejor sakori kiyo koribo bisarise?)
Candidate :	I have interest in teaching.	প্ৰাৰ্থী ঃ	শিক্ষকতাত মোৰ ৰাপ আছে। (xikhyokotat mor rap ase)
Office :	Only interest or any other reason, too?	বিষয়া ঃ	কেৱল ৰাপেইনে আৰু আন কিবা কাৰণো আছে ? (kewol rapeine aru an kiba karona ase?
Candidate :	Along with interest I think that it is our duty to teach the new generation.	প্ৰাৰ্থী ঃ	ৰাপৰ উপৰিও, মই ভাবোঁ যে নতুন পুৰুষক শিক্ষাদান কৰাটো আমাৰ এটা কৰ্তব্য। (rapor uprio, moi bhabo je notun puruxok xikhyadan korato amar

		aeta kortobyo.)
Officer :	Have you taught anywhere before?	বিষয়া ঃআপুনি আগতে ক'ৰবাত পঢ়ুৱাইছে নেকি ? (apuni agote korbat porhuwaise neki?)
Candidate :	Yes sir, after completing my B.Ed. I worked as a language teacher for four years in a school.	প্ৰাৰ্থী ঃ হয়, মহাশয়। বি.এড কৰাৰ পাছত মই চাৰিবছৰ এখন স্কুলত ভাষা শিক্ষক ৰূপে কাম কৰিছিলো। (hoi, mohaxoi, bi. ed korar pasot moi sari bosor aekhon skulot bhaxa xikhyok rupe kam korisilo.)
Officer :	Did you pass your M.A. while in teaching?	বিষয়া ঃআপুনি শিক্ষকতা কৰি থাকিয়েই এম.এ. পাছ কৰিছে নেকি ? (apuni xikhyokota kori thakiyei em. e. pass korise neki?)
Candidate :	Yes, sir Because I wanted to progress.	প্ৰাৰ্থী ঃ হয়, মহাশয়। কাৰণ মই উন্নতি কৰিব বিচাৰিছিলো। (hoi, mohaxoi, karon moi unnoti korib bisarisilo.)
Officer :	Very good.	বিষয়া ঃবৰ ভাল কথা। (bor bhal kotha.)

Candidate :	I am determined to do Ph.D.	প্ৰাৰ্থী ঃ	মই পি এইচ ডি কৰিম বুলি স্হিৰ কৰিছোঁ। (moi pi eich di korim buli sthir koriso)
Officer :	Well, Mr. Dutta; we shall inform you in time	বিষয়া ঃ	ভাল বাৰু মিষ্টাৰ দত্ত, আমি আপোনাক যথাসময়ত জনাম। (bhal baru mistar dotto, ami aponak jotha xomoyot jonam)
Candidate :	Thank you, sir.	প্ৰাৰ্থী ঃ	ধন্যবাদ, মহাশয়। (dhonyobad, mohaxoi)

FINANCIAL MATTERS
বিত্ত সম্পৰ্কীয় কথা-বতৰা
(bitto xomporkiyo kotha-botora)

Mr. Bora :	Come, come, how do you do?	শ্ৰীবৰা ঃ	আহক, আহক, কেনে আছে ? (ahok, ahok, kaenae ase?)
Miss Pronoti :	I am O.K., by your grace.	মিছ.প্ৰণতি ঃ	আপোনাৰ কৃপাত ভালেই আছো। (aponar kripat bhalei aso)
Bora :	Did you hear	বৰা ঃ	আপুনি কথা এটা

	something?		শুনিছেনে ? (apuni kotha aeta xunisene?)
Pronoti :	About what?	প্ৰণতি ঃ	কি কথা ? (ki kotha?)
Bora :	Don't you know that Dr. Chaudhury has got the prize?	বৰা ঃ	আপুনি নাজানে নেকি যে ডঃ চৌধুৰীয়ে পুৰস্কাৰ পাইছে ? (apuni najane neki jae doctor choudhuriye puroskar paise?)
Pronoti :	Oh, has he? It is really a matter of pleasure	প্ৰণতি ঃ	অ' হয় নেকি ? এইটো সঁচাই বৰ আনন্দৰ কথা । (hoi neki? eito xonsai bor anondor kotha.)
Bora :	Yes, it goes well for a writer.	বৰা ঃ	হয়, এজন লেখকৰ বাবে এইটো বৰ ভাল কথা । (khoi, aejon lekhokor babe eito bor bhal kotha)
Pronoti :	Now his financial position will also improve to some extent.	প্ৰণতি ঃ	এতিয়া তেওঁৰ আৰ্থিক অৱস্থাও কিছু উনত হ'ব । (etiya teonr arthik awosthao kisu unnoto hobo.)
Bora :	See, how a nice man also suffers because of want of money.	বৰা ঃ	চাওকচোন, টকা-পইচাৰ অভাৱত ভাল মানুহ এজনেও কেনেকৈ কষ্ট

			ভোগ কৰিবলগীয়া হয়। (saokson, toka-poisar abhawot bhal manuh aejoneo kenekoi kosto bhog koribologiya hoi)
Pronoti :	With what difficulty he was passing his days!	প্ৰণতি ঃ	কি কষ্টেৰে যে তেওঁ দিন কটাইছিল ! (ki kostere je teon din kotaisil!)
Bora :	The condition of his wife and children was miserable.	বৰা ঃ	তেওঁৰ পৰিবাৰ আৰু ল'ৰা-ছোৱালী কেইটাৰ অৱস্থা অতি দুখলগা হৈছিলগৈ। (teonr poribar aru lora-sowali keitar awostha oti dukh loga hoisilgoi)
Pronoti :	We had been neighbours for a long time.	প্ৰণতি ঃ	আমি বহুদিন ধৰি তেওঁলোকৰ প্ৰতিবেশী আছিলো। (ami bohudin dhori teonlokor protibexi asilo.)
Bora :	Everyone likes him for his amiable nature and his honesty.	বৰা ঃ	তেওঁৰ অমায়িক স্বভাৱ আৰু সততাৰ বাবে তেওঁক সকলোৱে ভাল পায়। (teonr omayik swobhaw

			aru xototar karone teonk xokolowe bhal pai)
Pronoti :	His play has also been staged.	প্ৰণতি ঃ	তেওঁৰ নাটকখনো মঞ্চস্থ কৰা হৈছে । (teonr natok khono monchostho kora hoise.)
Bora :	Yes, I went to see it. It was praised much in the newspapers also.	বৰা ঃ	অঁ, মই সেইখন চাবলৈ গৈছিলো । বাতৰি কাকতেও নাটকখনৰ খুব প্ৰশংসা কৰিছে । (on, moi xeikhon saboloi goisilo. batori kakot boreo natokkhonor khub proxongxa korise.)
Pronoti :	At last man's labour is rewarded.	প্ৰণতি ঃ	অৱশেষত এজন মানুহৰ পৰিশ্ৰম সাৰ্থক হ'ল । (owoxexot aejon manuhor porisrom xarthok hol.)
Bora :	You will see, one day this man will bring fame to the country.	বৰা ঃ	আপুনি চাব, এদিন এই মানুহজন দেশলৈ সুনাম কঢ়িয়াই আনিব । (apuni sabo, edin ei manuhjone dexoloi xunam korhiyai anibo.)

Pronoti : I consider him to be a great writer today itself.

প্ৰণতি ঃ মই তেওঁক এতিয়াই এজন মহান লেখক বুলি ভাবোঁ । (moi teonk etiyai aejon mohan lekhok buli bhabon)

Bora : You go and congratulate him. I had been to him today.

বৰা ঃ আপুনি তেওঁক অভিনন্দন জনাই আহকগৈ । মই আজি তেওঁৰ ওচৰলৈ গৈছিলো । (apuni teonk obhinondon jonai ahok goi. moi aji teonr osoroloi goisilo.)

Pronoti : Well, I'll also go today.

প্ৰণতি ঃ হয়, ময়ো আজি যাম । (hoi, moyo aji jam)

Bora : How pleasing it is to see some familiar one's name rising to the fame!

বৰা ঃ চিনাকি মানুহ এজনৰ নাম বিখ্যাত হৈ পৰিলে কিমান ভাল লাগে ! (sinaki manuh aejonor nam bikhyat hoi porile kiman bhal lage!)

Pronoti : Well, now I shall move. Thanks for the information.

প্ৰণতি ঃ বাৰু মই এতিয়া যাওঁ । খবৰটো দিয়াৰ কাৰণে ধন্যবাদ । (baru, moi etiya jaon. khoborto diyar karone dhonyobad)

Bora :	O.K., see you!	বৰা ঃ	আচ্ছা, লগ পাম। (achchha, log pam.)

DAY-TO-DAY DIFFICULTIES
দৈনন্দিন সমস্যা
(doinondin xomsya)

Kandarpa :	Hallo pradip, how are you?	কন্দৰ্প ঃ	হেল্ল' প্ৰদীপ ! কেনে আছা ? (haello prodip! kaenae asa?)
Pradip :	Don't ask anything. The shape of things is very bad due to inflation.	প্ৰদীপ ঃ	নক'বা আৰু। মুদ্ৰাস্ফীতিৰ কাৰণে একেবাৰে অৱস্থা বেয়া। (nokoba aru. mudrasfitin karone aekaebare owostha beya.)
Kandarpa :	Yes, yes. Every commodity has become dearer.	কন্দৰ্প ঃ	এৰা, ঠিকেই কৈছো। চব বস্তুৰে দাম বাঢ়ি গৈছে। (aera, thikei koisa. sob bosture dam barhi goise.)
Pradip :	The price of ghee and oil is not coming down.	প্ৰদীপ ঃ	ঘি আৰু তেলৰ দাম তো নকমাই হ'ল। (ghee aru taelor dam to nokomai hol)

Kandarpa :	In spite of the fact that government has taken stern measures, the result in nil.	কন্দৰ্প ঃ	চৰকাৰে কঠোৰ ব্যৱস্হা লোৱা সত্ত্বেও একো সুফল পোৱা নগ'ল । (sorkare kothor byowostha lowa sotteo aeko xuphol powa nogol)
Pradip :	How long will it go like this?	প্ৰদীপ ঃ	এইদৰে আৰু কিমান দিন চলিব ? (eidore aru kimandin solibo)
Kandarpa :	In my view, this rise and fall is seasonal. It will be alright after sometime.	কন্দৰ্প ঃ	মই ভাবোঁ এই উঠা-নমাটো সময় সাপেক্ষ । অলপদিনৰ পাছত চব ঠিক হৈ যাব । (moi bhabon ei utha-namato xomoi xapekhyo. olopdinor pasot sob thik hoi jabo)
Pradip :	Do you think so? Have the rates ever come down after rising?	প্ৰদীপ ঃ	তুমি তেনেকৈ ভাবা নেকি ? বস্তুৰ দাম এবাৰ বঢ়াৰ পাছত কেতিয়াবা কমা দেখিছা জানো ? (tumi tenekoi bhaba neki? bostur dam aebaar borhaar pasot ketiyaba koma dekhisa jano?)

Kandarpa :	Yes, it is so.	কন্দৰ্প ঃ	অঁ, সেইটো হয় পিছে। (on, xeito hoi pise)
Pradip :	Poverty and unemployment are not letting our country to prosper.	প্ৰদীপ ঃ	দাৰিদ্ৰ আৰু নিবনুৱা সমস্যাৰ কাৰণেই আমাৰ দেশৰ উন্নতি হোৱা নাই। (daridro aru nibonua xomosyar karonei amar dexor unnoti howa nai)
Kandarpa :	Isn't there any solution for it?	কন্দৰ্প ঃ	ইয়াৰ কোনো সমাধান নাই নেকি বাৰু ? (iyar kono xomadhan nai neki baru?)
Pradip :	We should limit our need.	প্ৰদীপ ঃ	আমি আমাৰ প্ৰয়োজনবোৰ সীমিত কৰা উচিত। (ami amar proyojonbor ximito kori usit)
Kandarpa :	Countless people are unemployed. How for can they limit their need?	কন্দৰ্প ঃ	অসংখ্য মানুহ নিবনুৱা হৈ আছে। তেওঁলোকে নিজৰ প্ৰয়োজন বিলাক কেনেকৈ সীমিত কৰিব ? (oxonkhyo manuh nibonua hoi ase. teonloke nijor proyojonbilak kaenaekoi ximito koribo?)
Pradip :	Yes, this is a	প্ৰদীপ ঃ	হয়, এইটো এটা জ্বলন্ত

	burning problem.		সমস্যা । (hoi, eito aeta jwolonto xomosya.)
Kandarpa :	And a challenge for us.	কন্দৰ্প ঃ	আৰু আমাৰ বাবে এটা প্ৰত্যাহবান। (aru amar babe aeta protyabhan)
Pradip :	It can be overcome only by discipline.	প্ৰদীপ ঃ	কেৱল অনুশাসনৰ দ্বাৰাহে এই সমস্যাৰ সমাধান কৰিব পৰা যায়। (kewol onuxaxonor dwarahe ei xomosyar xomadhan koribo pora jai.)
Kandarpa :	What you say is right, but empty boxes and canisters make the heart lose.	কন্দৰ্প ঃ	তোমাৰ কথাটো সঁচা; পিছে ঘৰৰ তলি উদং দেখিলে সাহস পলাই যায়। (tomar kotha xonsa, pise ghoror toli udong dekhile xahox polai jai.)
Pradip :	The only remedy is 'Curtail expenses and make both ends meet.'	প্ৰদীপ ঃ	একমাত্ৰ উপায় হ'ল– 'খৰচ কমোৱা আৰু কোনোমতে কাম চলোৱা।' (aekmatro upai hol 'khoros komowa aru konomote kam

			solowa.')
Kandarpa :	O.K.; friend, I'll make a move now. I have to purchase some articles.	কন্দৰ্প ঃ	আচ্ছা বন্ধু, মই এতিয়া যাওঁ। মই কেইটামান বস্তু কিনিব লাগে। (achcha bondhu, moi etiya jaon. moi keitaman bostu kinibo lage)
Pradip :	O.K.; see you again.	প্ৰদীপ ঃ	আচ্ছা, আকৌ লগ পাম। (achcha, akou log pam)

15. VISITING A PATIENT

এজন ৰোগীক দেখা কৰা

(aejon rogik daekha kora)

Jaya :	Where is ward No. two?	জয়া ঃ	দুই নম্বৰ ৱাৰ্ড কোনফালে ? (dui nombor ward konphale?)
Staff :	Go straight and turn left.	কৰ্মচাৰী ঃ	পোনে পোনে গৈ বাওঁফালে। (pone pone goi baonphale)
Jaya :	Thanks.	জয়া ঃ	ধন্যবাদ। (dhonyobad.)

Rekha :	Come, come	ৰেখা ঃ	আহা, আহা। (aha, aha)
Jaya :	How is your father now?	জয়া ঃ	তোমাৰ দেউতা এতিয়া কেনে আছে ? (tomar deuta etiya kaenae ase?)
Rekha :	He is better than before.	ৰেখা ঃ	আগতকৈ কিছু ভাল পাইছে। (agotkoi kisu bhal paise)
Jaya :	Who is treating him?	জয়া ঃ	তেখেতৰ চিকিৎসা কোনে কৰিছে ? (tekhetor sikitsa kone korise?)
Rekha :	Dr nath. He is a heart specialist.	ৰেখা ঃ	ডক্তৰ নাথে। তেওঁ এজন হৃদৰোগ বিশেষজ্ঞ। (doctor nathe. teon aejon hridrog bixexogyo.)
Jaya :	For how many days has your father been in the hospital?	জয়া ঃ	তোমাৰ দেউতা কিমান দিন ধৰি হস্পিটালত আছে ? (tomar deuta kiman din dhori hospitalot ase?)
Rekha :	Twenty days. First four-five days were very critical.	ৰেখা ঃ	বিশ দিন। প্ৰথম চাৰি-পাঁচ দিন যথেষ্ট সঙ্কটৰ মাজেদি পাৰ হ'ল। (bis din. prothom sari pans din jothesto

			xongkotor majedi par hol.)
Jaya :	Now, what does Dr. Nath say? How many more days will he have to stay here?	জয়া ঃ	এতিয়া ডঃ নাথে কি কয় ? আৰু কিমান দিন তেখেত ইয়াত থাকিব লাগিব ? (etiya doctor nathe ki koi? aru kiman din tekhet iyat thakibo lagibo?)
Rekha :	Only yesterday I had a talk with Dr. Nath It will take another ten days.	ৰেখা ঃ	মই কালি ডঃ নাথৰ লগত কথা পাতিছিলো । আৰু দহদিন থাকিব লাগিব হেনো । (moi kali doctor nathor logot kotha patisilo. aru dohdin thakibo lagibo haeno.)
Jaya :	Are you satisfied with Dr. Nath's treatment? Dr. Phukan is also here.	জয়া ঃ	তুমি ডঃ নাথৰ চিকিৎসাত সন্তুষ্ট নে ? ডঃ ফুকনো ইয়াতে আছে । (tumi doctor nathor (sikitsat xontustone? doctor phukono iyate ase.)
Rekha :	Yes, he also came to see. When my father was in intensive care unit,	ৰেখা ঃ	আঁ, তেৰোঁ আহিছিল চাবলৈ । দেউতা যেতিয়া ইন্টেনচিভ কেয়াৰ ইউনিটত আছিল, তেতিয়া ডঃ ফুকন

	Dr. Phukan used to come with Dr. Nath.		ডঃ নাথৰ লগত আহিছিল। (on tewon ahisil saboloi. deuta jetiya intensive kear unitot asil, tetiya doctor phukon doctor nathor logot ahisil.)
Jaya :	Dr. Phukan treated my father when he had heart trouble.	জয়া ঃ	মোৰ দেউতাৰ হাৰ্টৰ অসুখ হওঁতে ডঃ ফুকনে চিকিৎসা কৰি ভাল কৰিছিল। (mor deutar harton oxukh hownte doctor phukone sikitsa kori bhal korisil.)
Rekha :	Yes, I to came to know, but I had been out of station those days.	ৰেখা ঃ	অঁ, ময়ো খবৰ পাইছিলো, কিন্তু মই সেইসময়ত বাহিৰত আছিলো। (on, moyo khobor paisilo, kintu moi xei xomoyot bahirot asilo)
Jaya :	Father just got cured. We were very much non plussed.	জয়া ঃ	দেউতা কোনোমতেহে বাচিছে। আমি তো একেবাৰে বিবুদ্ধিত পৰিছিলো। (deuta konomotehe basise. ami to aekaebare bibuddhit porisilo.)

Rekha :	It happens. We also became nervous, but now there is some relief.	ৰেখা ঃ	এনেকুৱা হয়েই। আমিও ভয় খাইছিলো, কিন্তু এতিয়া বিপদ পাৰ হৈ গৈছে। (enekua hoyei. amio bhoi khaisilo, kintu etiya bipod par hoi goise.)
Joya :	Don't worry. All will be well. Yes, let him take sufficient rest even after he gets well.	জয়া ঃ	চিন্তা নকৰিবা। চব ঠিক হৈ যাব। অঁ, কিন্তু ভাল হৈ যোৱাৰ পাছতো তেখেতক যথেষ্ট জিৰণি ল'বলৈ দিবা। (sinta nokoriba. sob thik hoi jabo. on, kintu bhal hoi jowar pasoto tekhetok jothesto jironi laboloi diba.)
Rekha :	I will take care of it.	ৰেখা ঃ	মই এই কথাটোত চকু দিম। (moi ei kothatot soku dim.)
Jaya :	What food is being given to him?	জয়া ঃ	তেখেতক কি খাবলৈ দিছে ? (tekhetok ki khaboloi dise?)
Rekha :	Now the normal diet is being given. Father is not allowed to smoke	ৰেখা ঃ	এতিয়া স্বভাৱিক আহাৰ খাবলৈ দিছে। দেউতাৰ চিগাৰেট খোৱা বন্ধ। (eitya swabhavik ahar khaboloi dise. deutar sigaret khowa bondho.)

Jaya :	It was to be. Your father smoked heavily.	জয়া ঃ	সেইটো হ'বই। তোমাৰ দেউতাই খুব বেছি চিগাৰেট খাইছিল। (xeito hoboi. tomar deutai khub besi sigaret khaisil.)
Rekha :	This disease is the result of all that.	ৰেখা ঃ	তাৰেই ফল হ'ল এই বেমাৰটো। (tarei phol hol ei baemarto.)
Jaya :	Anything I can do?	জয়া ঃ	মোৰ কাৰণে কিবা কাম আছে নেকি ? (mo karone kiba kam ase neki?)
Rekha :	No; thanks for your visit.	ৰেখা ঃ	নাই, হ'ব দিয়া। তুমি অহাৰ কাৰণে ধন্যবাদ। (nai, hobo diya. tumi ohar karone dhonyobad.)
Jaya :	No Rekha, no formalities.	জয়া ঃ	নাই, ৰেখা, এইবোৰ ফৰ্মেলিটি কিয় ? (nai rekha, eibor formality kiyo?)
Rekha :	O.K. Jaya, Come again.	ৰেখা ঃ	বাৰু জয়া। আকৌ আহিবা, দেই। (baaru, joya. akou ahiba dei.)

16. AN ACCIDENT

এটা দুৰ্ঘটনা

(aeta durghotona)

Anil :	Hallo! Ashok, what's the matter? Why have so many people gathered here?	অনিল ঃ	অশোক, কি হ'ল ? ইয়াত ইমান মানুহ কিয় গোট খাইছে ? (ashok, ki hol? iyat iman manuh kiyo got khaise?)
Ashok :	A few minutes ago a bus and a motor cycle collided with each other.	অশোক ঃ	অলপ সময়ৰ আগতে এখন বাছ আৰু এখন মটৰ চাইকেলৰ মাজত খুন্দিয়া খুন্দি লাগিল। (olop xomoyor agote aekhon bas aru aekhon motor saikelor mazot khundia khundi lagil.
Anil :	But how did the accident take place?	অনিল ঃ	কিন্তু দুৰ্ঘটনাটো হ'ল কেনেকৈ ? (kintu durghotonato hol kaenaekoi?)
Ashok :	People are saying that the bus driver was drunk and was driving very rashly.	অশোক ঃ	মানুহে কৈছে যে বাছৰ ড্ৰাইভাৰে মদ খাই অসাৱধান ভাবে বাছ চলাইছিল।

(manuhe koise jue basordraivare mod khaioxawodhan bhabe gari solaisil.)

Anil : Then it was his fault. অনিল ঃ তেনেহ'লে তাৰ গাতেই দোষ।
(tenehole taar gaatei dox.)

Ashok : Yes; but the poor motorcycle rider.... অশোক ঃ অঁ, কিন্তু বেচেৰা মটৰ চাইকেল চলোৱা জন...
(on, kintu baesaera motor saikel solowajon...)

Anil : Why; is he hurt badly? অনিল ঃ কি, তেওঁ বেয়াকৈ আঘাত পালে নেকি ?
((ki, teon beyakoi aghat pale neki?)

Ashok : Yes, both his legs have been fractured. অশোক ঃ অঁ, তেওঁৰ দুয়োটা ভৰিয়েই ফ্রেকচাৰ হৈছে ।
(on, teonr duyota bhoriyei fraekchar hoise.)

Anil : Oh! that is very bad. Is the bus driver also hurt? অনিল ঃ অ' ! বৰ বেয়া কথা হ'ল। বাছ ড্রাইভাৰ জনেও আঘাত পাইছে নেকি ?
(oh! bor beya kotha hol. bas draivar joneo aghat

paise neki?)

Ashok : His head is injured. But fortunately there was no passenger in the bus

অশোক ঃ তেওঁ মূৰত দুখ পাইছে । কিন্তু সৌভাগ্যক্ৰমে বাছ-খনত কোনো যাত্ৰী নাছিল । (teon murot dukh paise, kinu xoubhagyo krome bas khonot kono jatri nasil.)

Anil : People are just watching instead of taking them both to the hospital.

অনিল ঃ দুয়োজনকে হস্পিটাললৈ লৈ নগৈ মানুহবোৰে কেৱল চাইহে আছে । (duyojonoke hospitaloloi loi nogoi manuhbore kewol saihae ase.)

Ashok : Who has the time? Then there is the problem of a witness.

অশোক ঃ সময়নো কাৰ হাত আছে ? ইফালে আকৌ সাক্ষী দিয়াৰ সমস্যাটো আছে নহয় । (xomoi no kaar hatot ase? iphale akou xakhyi diyar xomosyato ase nohai.)

Anil : That's true. Nowadays helping someone means—inviting trouble.

অনিল ঃ সেইটো হয় । আজিকালি কাৰোবাক সহায় কৰা মানে আপদ চপাই লোৱা । (xeito hoi. ajikali karobak xohai kora

mane—apod
sopai lowa.)

Ashok : You are right. There are crimes all around us, but nobody takes the initiative for fear of getting into trouble with police.

অশোক ঃ তুমি ঠিকেই কৈছা। আমাৰ চাৰিওপিনে অপৰাধ সংঘটিত হৈ আছে, কিন্তু পুলিচৰ লেঠাত সোমই পৰাৰ ভয়ত কোনো আগবাঢ়ি নাহে।
(tumi thikei koisa. amar sariopine aporadh xonghotito hoi ase, kintu pulisor lethat xomai porar bhoyot kono agbarhi nahe.)

Anil : And the youth of today doesn't like to drive below the speed of 70 km. They say they donot relish it

অনিল ঃ আৰু আজিকালিৰ ডেকা-ল'ৰাই সত্তৰ কিলোমিটাৰৰ তলত গাড়ী নচলায়েই। তেওঁলোকৰ মজাই নালাগে হেনো।
(aru ajikalir daeka lorai xottor kilomitaror tolot gari nosolayei. teonlokor haeno mozai nalage.)

Ashok : The main reason of road accidents is the driver's carelessness.

অশোক ঃ পথ দুৰ্ঘটনাৰ প্ৰধান কাৰণ হ'ল চালকৰ অসাৱধানতা।
(poth durghotonar

			prodhan karon hol salokor oxawodhanota.).
Anil :	And because of this carelessness so many deaths occur.	অনিল ঃ	আৰু এই অসাৱধানতাৰ কাৰণেই কিমান মানুহে যে প্ৰাণ হেৰুৱায়। (aru ei oxawodhanotar karonei kiman manuhe jae pran heruai.)
Ashok :	That is why I drive my scooter quite at a distance from trucks and buses.	অশোক ঃ	সেই কাৰণেই মই ট্ৰাক আৰু বাছৰ পৰা যথেষ্ট দূৰত্ব ৰাখি স্কুটাৰ চলাওঁ। (xei karonei moi trak aru basor pora jothesto durotto rakhi skutar salaon.)
Anil :	I have got the speed of my motor cycle fixed at 40 km per hour.	অনিল ঃ	মই মোৰ মটৰ চাইকেলৰ স্পীড প্ৰতি ঘণ্টাত চল্লিশ কিলোমিটাৰত বান্ধি ৰাখিছো। (moi mor motor saikaelor speed proti ghontat sollis kilomitarot bandhi rakhiso.)
Ashok :	The easiest way to avoid accident	অশোক ঃ	দুৰ্ঘটনাৰ পৰা হাত সৰাৰ আটাইতকৈ সহজ

is to obey traffic rules and to take precautions while driving.

উপায় হ'ল যাতায়াতৰ নিয়মবোৰ মানি চলা আৰু গাড়ী চলোৱাৰ সময়ত সাৱধানতা অৱলম্বন কৰা।
(durghotonar pora hat xorar ataitkoi xohoz upai hol jatayator niyombor manisola aru gari solowar xomoyot xawodhanota owolombon kora)

nil : You are right. Well, now let's take both of them to the hospital without wasting more time.

অনিল ঃ তুমি ঠিকেই কৈছা। আচ্ছা, এতিয়া আৰু সময় নষ্ট নকৰি দুয়োজনকে হস্পিটাললৈ লৈ যাওঁ ব'লা।
(tumi thikei koisa. achchha, etiya aru xomoi nosto nokori duyojonoke hospitaloloi loi jawn bola.)

17. ON THE RAILWAY PLATFORM
ৰে’লৱে’ প্লেটফৰ্মত
(reilway plaetformot)

Pass. 1 :	(To Cooli) Where is platform no. 4?	১ম যাত্ৰী ঃ	চাৰি নম্বৰ প্লেটফৰ্ম কোনফালে ? (sari nombor platform kon phale?)
Kuli :	Across the overbridge to the right.	কুলী ঃ	অ’ভাৰব্ৰিজ পাৰ হৈ সোঁফালে । (ovarbrij par hoi xon phole.)
Pass. 1 :	What is your coach number?	১ম যাত্ৰী ঃ	আপোনাৰ ক’চ নম্বৰ কিমান ? (aponar coch nombor kiman?)
Pass. 2 :	S-2, and yours?	২য় যাত্ৰী ঃ	এচ-টু । আৰু আপোনাৰ ? (es-tu. aru aponar?)
Pass. 1 :	I am also in the same coach. It's very nice. We shall be together and the journey won't be boring.	১ম যাত্ৰী ঃ	ময়ো সেইটো ডবাতেই আছোঁ । ভালেই হ’ল । আমি একেলগেই যাম; আৰু যাত্ৰাটো আমনিদায়ক নহ’ব । (moyo xeito dobatei aso. bhalei hol. ami aekelogei jam, aru

		jatrato amoni dayok nohobo.)
Pass. 2 : How long will the train take to reach Guwahati?	২য় যাত্ৰী ঃ	গাড়ী গুৱাহটী গৈ পাওঁতে কিমান সময় লাগিব ? (gari guwahati goi pawnte kiman xomoi lagibo?)
Pass. 1 : 36 hours. It's a nearly two thousand kilometres journey.	১ম যাত্ৰী ঃ	৩৬ ঘণ্টা। প্ৰায় দুহেজাৰ কিলোমিটাৰৰ যাত্ৰা। (soitris ghonta. prai duhezar kilomitaror jatra.)
Pass. 2 : Youhave only one attache?	২য় যাত্ৰী ঃ	আপোনাৰ লগত মাত্ৰ এটাই এটাচি আছে ? (aponar logot matro aetai atachi ase?)
Pass. 1 : Yes, sir. I like to travel with minimum baggage.	১ম যাত্ৰী ঃ	হয়, মহাশয়। মই যিমান মই যিমান পাৰি কম বস্তু লগত লৈ যাত্ৰা কৰো। (hoi mohaxoi. moi jiman pari kom bostu logot loi jatra koro)
Pass. 2 : Are you going on a pleasure trip or do you live there?	২য় যাত্ৰী ঃ	আপুনি ফুৰিবলৈ যায় নে তাতে থাকে ? (apuni phuriboloi jai ne tate thake?)
Pass. 1 : Yes, I live there	১ম যাত্ৰী ঃ	হয়, মই তাতে থাকোঁ–

	at Chandmari. I own a business there.		চাঁদমাৰীত। তাত মোৰ ব্যৱসায় আছে। (hoi, moi tate thako. sandmarit. taat mor byowoxai ase.)
Pass. 2 :	I am going there for the first time. Would you please suggest me some places of tourist interest?	২য় যাত্ৰী ঃ	মই তালৈ এয়া প্ৰথমবাৰ যাম। আপুনি মোক তাৰ চাবলগীয়া ঠাই কিছুমানৰ নাম ক'ব পাৰিবনে ? (moi taaloi eya prothombar jam. apuni mok taar sabologia thai kisumanor nam kobo paribone?
Pass. 1 :	Certainly, and I'd be glad to accompany you there once or twice.	১ম যাত্ৰী ঃ	নিশ্চয়। আৰু মই তাত আপোনাক দুই-এদিন লগ দিব পাৰিলে আনন্দিত হ'ম। (nissoi, aru moi taat aponak dui-edin log dibo parile anondito hom.)
Pass. 2 :	Thanks. But I don't want to trouble you. There are one or two friends of mine.	২য় যাত্ৰী ঃ	ধন্যবাদ। কিন্তু মই আপোনাক কস্ট দিব নোখোজো। তাত মোৰ দুজনমান বন্ধু আছে। পিছে মই তাত

	But I'd like to see you there. Then we can chalkout a programme.		আপোনাকো লগ কৰিব বিচাৰো, তেতিয়া আমি এটা ভ্ৰমণ-সূচী তৈয়াৰ কৰি ল'ব পাৰিম। (dhonyobad, kintu moi aponak kosto kibo nokhojo. taat mor dujonman bondhu ase. pise moi taat aponako log koribo bisaro; tetiya ami aeta bhromon-xusi toiyar kori lobo parim.)
Pass. 1 :	O.K., as you please.	১ম যাত্ৰী ঃ	ঠিক আছে। আপুনি যি কয়। (thik ase. apuni ji koi.)
Pass. 2 :	Please tell me your address in Guwahati.	২য় যাত্ৰী ঃ	অনুগ্ৰহ কৰি মোক আপোনাৰ গুৱাহাটীৰ ঠিকনাটো দিয়ক চোন। (onugroh kori mok aponar guwahatir thikonato diyok son.)
Pass. 1 :	We have to travel a long way. I shall give you my address and the phone number in the train.	১ম যাত্ৰী ঃ	আমি বহুত দূৰ যাত্ৰা কৰিব লাগিব। মই আপোনাক ট্ৰেনেতে মোৰ মোৰ ঠিকনা আৰু ফোন নম্বৰ দি দিম।

		(ami bohut door jatra karibo lagibo. moi aponak treinote mor thikona aru phon nombor di dim.)
Pass. 2 : Well, let's have some cold drinks. It's very hot today and there is still half an hour till the train leaves.	২য় যাত্ৰী ঃ	আহক, অলপ ক'ল্ড ড্ৰিংকচ খাওঁ। আজি বৰ গৰম পৰিছে, ইফালে ট্ৰেইন এৰিবলৈ তো এতিয়াও আধা ঘন্টা আছে। (ahok, olop cold drinks khaon. aji bor gorom porise; iphale trein eriboloi to etiyao adha ghonta ase.)
Pass. 1 : O.K.; Lets move!	১ম যাত্ৰী ঃ	ঠিক আছে, ব'লক। (thik ase; bolok.)

• • •